Philip Pearson

A Challenger's Song

AUSTIN MACAULEY PUBLISHERS™

LONDON • CAMBRIDGE • NEW YORK • SHARJAH

Book Design by Russell Holden  Pixel Tweaks Publications
www.pixeltweakspublications.com   SELF PUBLISHING MADE SIMPLE

Cover Design by Nick Grant
www.nickgrantillustrator.com

The author gratefully acknowledges the support from the *Challenger* Council towards the publication of this book.

A CIP catalogue record for this title is available from the British Library.

ISBN 9781398473713 (Paperback)
ISBN 9781398473720 (ePub e-book)

www.austinmacauley.com

First Published 2021
Austin Macauley Publishers Ltd®
1 Canada Square
Canary Wharf
London E14 5AA

For Nony

Contents

PART ONE

Charlie Collins – One of the *Challenger's* Crew

PART TWO
The *Challenger* Expedition (1872-1876)

PART THREE

The Sea Never Let Him Go

Songs

Preface

'Old Grandad Collins ran away to sea without his family's sanction,' so his granddaughter, my mother Stella, once told me. On New Year's Day 1863, aged fourteen, he set off from Brighton, his home town, for Portsmouth to join the Royal Navy. In 1872, he sailed to the South Pole, she said, as a crewman on HMS *Challenger* 'with the Nares-Thomson expedition.' *Challenger* undertook the greatest scientific voyage of its time, laying the foundations of the scientific study of the sea. She was powered by sail and steam and Charlie Collins was the leading stoker.

A Challenger's Song is in three parts. The first reimagines Charlie's restless life on ship and ashore, drawing on our family's oral history, incidents in fellow sailors' diaries and archive materials. In 1876, on *Challenger*'s triumphant return to Chatham Docks, Charlie left the Navy. But although he 'swallowed the anchor' that day, a seaman's habits would never let him go. During his many 'disappearances,' perhaps on the drink or back on a ship, his hardworking, intelligent wife, Mary, would fend for their growing family.

The second part tells afresh the extraordinary story of the *Challenger* expedition through the eyes of the crew and scientists who sailed with her, drawing on their letters and accounts.

In all weathers, the crew sounded and dredged 'the great ocean basins' to retrieve thousands of unknown species. They charted new telegraph routes and wherever they landed, were instructed to study the flora and fauna and observe the 'native races' they might encounter. The expedition's mammoth Report laid the foundations for the new science of oceanography.

Part Three provides a biography of Charlie's life and times, drawing on Royal Navy, census, newspaper and other archives. Neither Charlie's letters nor other written account of his voyage remains. Yet the course, contradictions and kindnesses of his life endured in the memories of his grandchildren, for a remembered phrase, gesture or event can uniquely reveal aspects of a person beyond the reach of any records.

The narrative makes frequent references to sea shanties, for these songs convey much more of the life of a sailor in those times than any report or ship's log. Some original songs inspired by the mariners' stories are reproduced in the final part of the book.

- Part One -

Charlie Collins
One of the *Challenger's* Crew

Able Seaman Charlie Collins (1847-1932)

HMS *Challenger* under sail, 1874: *Challenger* Report.

Collision

February 1874

Oh, the Southern Ocean is a lonely place,
Where the storms are many and the shelter scarce,
Down upon the Southern Ocean sailing,
Down below Cape Horn.

'Mollymawk,' Bob Watson

To mark the *Challenger's* first crossing of the Antarctic Circle, Captain George Nares, one of the greatest surveyors in the Royal Navy, orders wine to be issued to officers, scientists and crew alike. He cordially invites Professor Wyville Thomson, who heads the team of six scientists, to lead the toast. They've now reached deep into the Southern Ocean, a lonely place, where the storms are many and the shelter scarce. All men are in their Navy-issued Polar slops - large caps with flaps to cover the ears, great jackets, trousers, boots and mittens. It's 10 pm and the sun is still above the horizon, with the sky lit like fire.

Joe Matkin, assistant steward, turns again to his letter writing, pen in hand, in the fug and warmth of the stove in the Issuing Room, three decks down. The last of the sun is 'giving all the bergs to the west a scarlet tinge,' he writes to his mother, 'and there's any amount of great Whales in sight, all blowing & having a game among themselves.'

Challenger's eastward course was then much impeded by the great lumps of floating ice and the roar they made thumping against the bows of the vessel in the night. 'I shall never forget it,' Joe writes. 'It was like thunder more than anything else and the grinding noise woke all who were in their hammocks, and nearly everyone went on deck. It was a beautiful sight to see the ship ploughing her way through, and the light emitted from the ice made it nearly as light as day. The light is called by polar voyagers, Ice Blink.'

'At midnight it was light enough to see and read, and the sky was still scarlet in the west where the sun had gone down.'

On 19 February, the ship passes any number of bergs looking, to Joe's mind, like the Chalk Cliffs of Dover. But five days later, as soon as the scientists' dredging gear came up out the water, it comes on to blow and all hands are called to make sail away for Melbourne. The captain, with his Arctic experience, is inclined to force his way through the outer ice barrier and penetrate further South, but his instructions from the Admiralty forbid him. He doesn't want to end up ice bound in the Antarctic, driven to eating his boots like poor old Sir John Franklin. And as the steward's assistant well knows, 'We have only three months provisions & 80 tons of coal left on the ship.'

There's a fierce snowstorm building, the ship now steaming close under the protective lee of a large berg to allow the topsails to be reefed, but some undercurrent is urging her right on to the berg. And as the captain hollers 'Full speed astern,' Assistant Chief Engineer William Spry cries, 'Full astern! All boilers full steam. Look bloody handy.'

Even as he's yelling, they are throwing coals into the four boilers. Spry closes down the throttle, the screws slow painfully to idling, and he must stay his trembling hand, waiting for that sweet spot somewhere between his expertise and a prayer, when he can risk reversing the temperamental 400 horsepower engine. He knows he must move quickly, but this is no lubber's docking manoeuvre. And as he chooses his moment to pull the reverse linkage over, the whole vessel rattles and shakes in the propeller's turbulence. The shaft is mere metal bolted to wood, the Southern Ocean vast, waiting to receive.

As the ship rises and falls in the heavy swell, the screws slow then strain and churn then eat into their own wake, the reverse pull heading for sixty revolutions a minute and more. Down in the engine room, pistons screech and pound, regulators spin in a blur, coal stacks slide across the stoking room floor, the air heavy with coal dust and cursing.

And as Charlie bends his back to shovel black coal into the boiler's roaring, hungry red mouth, heave and turn, heave and turn, for full steam was the orders, he thinks of home. And in the insane intensity of his labour prowls a recurring anger. His father's crimson face screaming back at him above the roar and red of the furnace door.

You'll work with me.

I won't

Get out, then! You little bastard. Get out!

Just watch me!

Well, he'd got out. Got out.

'Easy, Mr Collings, I think that's enough. Stand easy, Charlie, stand easy.'

Charlie draws a damp grey rag across his brow, plunges his pint tin into the pail of ice cold water, drinks and spits out a mouthful of black phlegm and pours the rest over his boiling brain. Takes a second swallow as the engineer is slamming the door on the last of the four boilers, all now at full steam. The corvette shudders violently in the pulling back and pounding back of the screws into their own wild churning wake.

'It don't have enough power.'

'I told them we'd need more,' says the engineer.

And lifted on the swell, the ship bumps and smashes into the berg, spearing the ice with its jib boom and forward gear. The stokers below sway with the impact while the men aloft, thinking they would have the top gallant mast about their ears, scurry down with marvellous activity, and the captain and commander howling out orders from the bridge, hardly heard in the roaring of the wind, and the officers repeating the howls.

The prow is a wreck. In the boiler hold they hear the ice fist-thumping against the oak, but the hull, after all, isn't breached.

Challenger archive, Natural History Museum.

Boy Sailor, Portsmouth

1 JANUARY 1863

'Remember what we said now, Charlie, if they ask. Father gave permission.'

Charlie Collings follows his uncle Henry to meet the Navy recruitment board, assembled for another day's work in the Admiralty's administration block overlooking Number 2 dock, Portsmouth. It's the biggest room he's ever been in. The four-teen-year-old looks out at the rain still thrashing against the high windows, a blur of masts swaying beyond. The clerk, stiff white collar, motions his uncle to a seat by the wall, and Charlie, short but stocky of stature, stands before the three-man panel. Coals blaze in the hearth behind their backs. A Nelson in oils leans over the high mantle. The lad twists a damp cloth cap behind his back, for they were caught in a squall on their way from the harbour station.

Retired Captain Robert Cooke, his jacket uncomfortably tight, sits between Medical Officers William Smythe and Belgrave Nimins.

'And you are Charles Collings, is that right?'

'Yes, Sir.'

'Born 18 August 1848, correct?'

'Sir.' For he believes it to be so.

The three officers are appointed under Admiralty Regulations with examining today's clutch of volunteer Boy Sailors. At stake is this boy's fitness in mind and body to enter Her Majesty's Royal Navy.

The captain glances at the form in front of him on the desk.

'Mr Henry Collings is here today to hand you over to us, is he?'

'Sir.'

'But we have your father down as a Matthewman, Charles Matthewman?'

'Now why then..?'

The boy grips his hat.

'...do you want to become a sailor in the Royal Navy of Queen Victoria? Can you swim, boy?'

'Yes, Sir. I'm from Brighton.'

'Father's occupation?'

'Plasterer, Sir.'

'Remove your tops, boy.'

Medical Officer Smythe gets up from behind the desk and leads the boy to a measuring stick by the wall, looks him in the eyes.

'Make a note,' he says to the clerk. 'We have five feet and a quarter inches. Hazel eyes, I'd say. Dark brown hair. Dark complexion. No marks that I can see. Turn round, lower your britches, will you. Well grown.'

'Dress yourself. Take your time. Now, are you desirous to be entered for 10 years' service in Her Majesty's Navy when you reach the age of 18?'

'I am, Sir.'

'Good. That's it. Perhaps you'd be kind enough, then, Mr Collings, to step forward and sign the boy's form. Here and here.'

His uncle duly certifies that: 'My son Charles, has my full consent (himself willing) to enter HM Navy for a period of Ten Years Continuous Service, from the age of 18, in addition to whatever period may be necessary to attain that age...'

A commitment to at least 13 years' service.

And addressing the boy, Captain Cooke says, 'From here you new boys will be rowed out to HMS *St Vincent*. Give you a bath. Fit you out with a set of clothes. You'll have a prayer and hymn book and a ditty bag for your things. Vaccinate you. Smallpox. You'll be taught the skills of a sailor. You're a Sailor Boy 2nd Class now. You'll salute me. That's it. Dismissed.'

Outside the room, with furrowed brow, his uncle looks at the boy, says, 'Straightaway you go, then?'

The boy swallows hard, says quietly, 'It's what I want.'

'I know it is, my dear. I'll see your father straight.'

And then, 'You'll be back home on leave in six months. We can get the boat out, do some proper sailing. There'll be plenty of mackerel about.'

Ellis Banfield, Brighton

JUNE 1863

It's midsummer, and after their first six months' induction, those new *St Vincent* trainees with a home to go to, such as Charlie, are allowed three weeks' leave. The orphan boys, and there are many, must remain on board ship. Early on this Saturday morning, young Ellis Banfield, Charlie's childhood friend, hurries along the seafront and cuts up into the back streets of Brighton's Kemp Town. He'd got away early. In truth, he should be mixing plaster with his father. But instead he slips along the shadowy back twittens joining the narrow streets, between high walls of pebble and flint, and raps on the back yard door.

Hearing his friend, Charlie lifts the latch. Ellis, a head taller, ducks under the door frame, and they stare at each other. It's been six months.

'You got a holy cross tattooed on your arm,' Ellis says. 'You weren't religious.'

'Let's go down the beach,' Charlie replies, and takes a cloth for each of them from his uncle Henry's back kitchen.

Charlie doesn't like to show it, but the salt water stings not just the freshly pinned tattoo, but the still raw welts across his back. In a few minutes, they're floating on the low surf, chucking water, diving to touch the sandy floor, bringing up a shell or a handful of seaweed. And back on the beach, one tosses a pebble in the air, the other aims a stone as it arches back into the sea. One connects with a crack. It's Charlie's, he's had small arms practice.

'We all gets the rope's end,' says Charlie, anticipating his friend's question. 'Instructors don't mind handing it out, right or left if you're in the way. But there ain't much I can't do already.'

And his friend, on his back, eyes closed to the low sun, says, 'Like what, then?'

'Well, everything and nothing. It's all a routine.' And he realises he's speaking with a sudden pride. 'They're bawling you out at half past five. Rouse out, show a leg and all that. Hammocks up, and a kick up the arse if you don't shift. Worst bit is when it's your turn to holystone the decks before we get breakfast, that's every other day. But then it's sail drills, that starts at eight. They sets up a yard arm across the deck, see, not high up, so if you fall off you don't hurt yourself. We're as shown how to get the sails in and out, loose and furl, over haul, all that. After that, they let us go aloft. Everyone wants to get right up to the cross trees. I ain't an upper yard boy yet, but I will be.'

Behind his eyes he remembers the first initiation, a thump on the back of his head from one the officer's sons. And he knew if he didn't return the compliment it would serve him no good. So he'd deadlegged the lad, driven his knee into a thigh.

'Then, the chaplain takes assembly, we say our prayers, all the new boys. Then it's more seamanship, like swimming, that's the easy bit, boat pulling, done that, knots and splices. Some of it's hard though, compass stuff, bearings.'

He yawns, drifts on. 'Another assembly at one, 'front of the captain this time, and then we gets our dinner. After that, clothes washing, tea at five, then cleaning the mess or washing the upper deck for the officers. Bit of supper, then free time. That's my day.'

'When do you go sailing, then?' Ellis wants to know.

Charlie rolls over, sits on his friend's chest, pins both Ellis's wrists against the stones and looks into his face. 'When I'm good and ready, mate,' he says. 'Got a pal, Thomas Holman, says the Navy's his wildest dream. It's alright.'

He stands astride his friend, feet splayed. 'I was up aloft there one day, see, and one of the boys was standing on the yard, that's a spar to you, across the other side of the mast, shivering and holding on to the rigging like grim death. His eyes was standing out of his head. Boy next to me, Patrick, got hold of his arm, to steady him like. Most of the other boys had gone down by then. And he says, now follow me, I'll show you the way. And we got him to stop a while by the lubber's hole up there, and when he's calmed himself, Patrick led him down. Shook our hands. He said it was the first time he'd been right up aloft.'

Charlie stretches his arms above his head, loosens his shoulders, turns to warm his back in the low sun.

'How many of you?' asks Ellis.

'Hundred, maybe. Why, you thinking of it?'

'No chance.'

'We get a Thursday afternoon ashore. Entertainments, bit of singing on a Saturday evening. Best dinner of the week Sundays, and a run ashore. No?'

Ellis realises he hasn't had plaster dust out of his hair all week.

And they're both swimming out again, the undulating sea parting sweetly as they cleave away. They're far out. They turn, float on their backs, resting, and look towards the beach and the town behind. There's the dark figure of a man standing by their pile of clothes. Ellis should be mixing plaster with his father.

Mary

JANUARY 1871

I'm bound away to leave you,
Shallow, Oh shallow brown
I never will deceive you,
Shallow, my shallow brown.

Traditional.

Dawn, but it could be any hour of this long January night. In the distance, St Bartholomew's church is striking six bells as the last railway carriage curves slowly out of sight, enveloping the trackside trees in a bluster of smoke. Mary Collins turns to walk back down the station platform, gathers the woollen shawl tight around her shoulders, as if to fend off the prowling thought, that she and Charlie have spent no more than a handful of days together since their marriage last May.

And for his past absconding, he was allowed just one day's leave this time. *You must, please, write to me, tell me how you are,* his urgent parting words.

Mary stands in the living room of the Laundry House, on the edge of town. She brushes out her auburn hair. Smoothing the front of her dress with a sideways glance at the mirror, she remembers that first fortnight of married life together here at Maresfield, just last May. Charlie arriving with the prize of two whole weeks' shore leave under his belt, the delights of their marriage on 15 May, a small gathering at St Bartholomew's. If his father was absent, well, the rose petals scattered such troubles on the breeze.

And the kit bag he'd flung so carelessly on top of their wardrobe. A heavy presence, for her, that bag, but she hadn't said. And besides, he'd claim that no hammock was a match for such a bed. The ravel and weave, she thought, of their first fortnight together, but then his leave tumbling to an end like a dropped cotton reel. Mary had heard him packing upstairs, turning about on the bare boards in their room above, running late, drawers sliding open, a wardrobe door banging to. Her going up.

'No, no I don't need your help.'

And, realising he was maybe too abrupt: 'I just need to make sure it's all packed in the right place.'

Then more gently, 'And I thank you for getting my blues and whites all clean and ready for me. But you can just walk with me to the station.'

She'd bitten back her reply – he'd be gone heaven knows how long and just these two suddenly short weeks together.

Handing him his sewing kit, she'd said, 'Don't forget your little housewife. You sailor boys. Everything has to be ship shape, doesn't it?'

Struggling to lighten the atmosphere.

'Orders is orders,' he'd said. 'I got to be back on *Penelope* come nightfall.'

'And I'm coming with you', she had replied, 'as far as London anyway.'

But his will prevailed, and by nightfall she was back home and he was clambering back aboard HMS *Penelope*.

Mary straightens the dried flowers of her wedding bouquet held in the small glass vase on their mantlepiece. What time have we had together? Those two stolen days in October, absent without leave, him arriving at dawn like a will o'the wisp. Impulsive as ever, and her day's work left untended. A letter followed, promising to return on 15 January, 'and then we're at sea for a good while.' But he was denied more than a single day.

She sees them walk in silence in step towards the station's yellowing light, the first people about, his bag over one shoulder, a warm arm linked into hers. The Maresfield line, change at Redhill, destination Deal on the Kent coast, where his ship now rides at anchor: these details she knows. Mary has her own train fare in her purse. He places the kit bag down on the platform and taking her hand, his hazel eyes meeting her blue, hers lowered now, misting, he says, 'We must say our goodbyes here my dear,' with no give in his voice. 'You will not want to be be coming back from Deal on your own.'

She turns away, walks down the platform, concealing the clench and unclench of her hands, in the silence of this early dawn before the din of the train will drown it all.

She returns to him, moves close, places her hand on his chest, looks up into his face. 'I think I'm with child, Charles,' she says.

'Keep an eye on our lad'

November 1872

Well you're looking mighty smart, boy
Dressed up in your number ones
You've scrounged a new blade from the purser
To take the bum-fluff from off your chin.

And one more pull boys, that'll do boys
Soon we'll draw alongside.
Hoist her up boys, swing her inboard
For the journey's nearly done.

'One more pull,' Ian Woods

'Next!' Able Seaman Collings gets up smartly from the bench, turns to grip the hand of the man he's just met, John Stokes, a Thames pilot, he tells him, and wearing a new pea jacket. In their short acquaintance, Charlie also learns that he is bringing his son, William, to claim a place among those boy sailors aspiring to join the *Challenger*.

Charlie stamps his way up the stone staircase to the surgeon's rooms directly overlooking No. 2 dock, Sheerness, where *Challenger* is being got ready for all to see, and comes to a halt, ready for his examination. The Admiralty clerk, who will amend the sailor's Certificate of Service, stands at a high wooden desk, ledger open, pen poised. Channelling his nerves, the seaman's attention is first caught by the sight of an 18-pound cannon now swinging away from the *Challenger's* gantry to the dock-side. The crew are unloading all but two of its 17 guns to make way for laboratories, storage and cabins for the scientists due on board. And now he stares at the hauling up of the brand new and tightly furled top gallants of the three-masted, steam-assisted corvette that he's aching to join come December.

For this day, and for the rest of the week, Staff Surgeons Crosbie and Maclean will divide between them an examination of the 240 ratings and able seamen and boys who may be shipped on board of the *Challenger*, subject to their good service and good health. For each sailor in turn, the clerk will record details of their personal identification and Naval service. The surgeons will want to know if they are carrying broken bones, bowel fluxes, fevers or grudges that won't heal. And the final decision will lie with Captain George S. Nares.

Charlie can't get the idea out of his head that the clerk is at a pulpit about to read a sermon. Staff Surgeon Crosbie eyes the short, stocky already balding young man before him. Snaps:

'Able Seaman Collings.'

'Sir.'

'We'll need to confirm a few personal details. Is that Collings with a "g".'

'Sir.'

'Unusual.'

'Sir.'

'Family from?'

'Brighton, Sir.'

'Make a note', says the surgeon,

'Now, six years as an Able Seaman, that right? And some more as a Boy?'

'Sir. Three as a Boy, Sir.'

And at the age of 24, with the *Challenger* now recruiting fourteen stokers for a voyage the like of which was never seen, he's on the short list for what he thinks will likely be his last, and by a mile the most lengthy venture.

Beckoning the seaman to stand back to a yardstick, Mr Crosbie dictates to the clerk:

'Height five feet, three and a half inches. Now open your eyes wide and look to the window. Eyes hazel. Hair brown. Complexion...'

The surgeon looks carefully at the man's pale, yellow skin, thinking without comment that it's the commonplace heavy smoking, if not the victuals, or the tell-tale of some fever overcome.

'Any fever still lingering on, Able Seaman?'

'None Sir.'

'Record that as complexion sallow.'

'And you'll be wanting to be a stoker?'

'Sir.'

'Do you have a trade, Collings?'

'Blacksmith, Sir'.

'Good. So, you'll be capable of iron work, on board, if the need arises, that it?'

'Sir.'

'Remove your slops, if you would be so kind, top first.'

The Able Seaman removes his cap and, crossing his arms, takes the hem of his thick, white cotton shift in each hand. It's over his head, and placed on the floor.

The surgeon walks round him. Notes the ship in a dark blue tattoo across a broad chest.

'Been round the Horn, I see. Who were you with?'

'Captain Thomson, Sir.'

'Mark this down please clerk. Ship on breast. I see a crucifix on right arm. Euridice on left. Bracelets on wrists.'

He looks at the man's physique.

'Would you just drop your kegs, no need to remove them.'

The move reveals a long patch of pink, ruffled skin from the seaman's right hip to his ankle.

'Burst steam pipe, Sir.'

'Healed well I see. Any impediment to your movement as a result?'

'None now Sir.'

'Broken bones?'

'None Sir.'

He turns to the clerk.

'What do we have on character?'

'Very good, in the report, doctor.'

'I see,' is all he says.

'Next.'

Collings salutes and turns, stamps out a smart about turn on the bare oak boards. About to depart the Admiralty building, pleased that the examination has gone without a hitch, he passes Stokes on the stair. The Deal pilot gently takes his elbow, and to one side, says quietly, 'If he succeeds, you'll keep an eye on our lad, our William, would you?'

'Aye, I will, sir.'

He nods, and in that moment between fathers, of course, sees again in his own arms his own son, John. It's pure chance, he knows that. Such reminders can come at you from any quarter, anytime. Best of all when your guard is down, like now, when something in your day might have gone well.

Collecting his bag from the shore-side mess room, and with the London train due in an hour, Charlie heads for the Railway Tavern. No longer seeking company, he takes his drink to one side, sits now engrossed in the silent memory of his last time home. Maresfield, June 1871, just after she had John. Family complete. Four whole days to greet, hold, christen and love their new born son. And then, come October, the mail delivered to *Penelope* bearing her letter to tell of their loss. Just four months old. The boy taken by a fever.

He stands, hoisting the bag over his shoulder.

He'll be at Maresfield by the end of the day. They'll have a week together, him and Mary.

'I must buy something for her in town first.'

Turkey bones

CHRISTMAS 1872

It's been six days out from Portsmouth since HMS *Challenger* threaded its way past the Needles, all hands saluting the Queen at Osborne House on the Isle of Wight. If the storm coming out of Sheerness was a bad enough omen, the ship soon ran into a fierce headwind down Channel, with stormy weather coming on and the ship rolling like mad. Captain's orders swung between either full steam, head to wind, or beating about under full sail. At its height, the storm added to its howling shrouds new verses of smashing crockery or the cabin groans of the six 'scientifics' still wanting their sea legs.

There's still a heavy swell even now. Charlie swallows a pint of water and heads up the ladderway for fresh sea air and five minutes' respite from the heat and dust kicked up by the restless coal. With the ship just going about yet again under full sail and the engine idling, he thinks he'll see if Joe Matkin, the assistant steward, is free. They first met in November, both watching her loading up while awaiting their surgeon's examination.

He looks into the issuing room.

'What you writing there, Joe?' Joe is younger, just 19, with still more bum fluff than beard on his chin, but he's got a nice look in his eye, even though he keeps himself to himself. It's his second ship. He's from a printing family, an habitual writer himself.

'It's to my mother. For posting when we gets to Lisbon.'

Charlie pauses by the high, standing desk. There's a single candle, its steady flame in a glass jar casting a pool of yellow light across the notepad. Joe dips his sharpened pen into a well of deep blue ink that moves with the roll and pitch of the ship. He taps the stylus with his stained index finger so the inky bulb drops economically back into the well, and he looks up.

'My father's not well, Charlie. Mother has enough on her plate without worrying about me too.'

Charlie stands watches his scribbling for a minute or two. 'Won't you join me on deck for a moment? It's awfully stuffy down here?'

Joe dries his pen, stretches his back. 'I see the cook has set a guard to watch on the kitchen.'

'Yesterday's turkey disappearing.'

'Aye, before it reached the captain's table. And never heard of since,' says Joe. 'Well, except for the bones and a bit of salt found this morning, tucked away in the tops'al'.

'All very mysterious.'

'They made a right kick up about it.'

'It's goose today, so I believe. A guarded goose.'

And pulling on his coat, Joe says, 'But them officers never go short. We still served them nice cuts of cold meat and pickle.'

'Lucks for them it wasn't a bit of hard biscuit.'

'Or salt pork.'

'Or pea soup.'

And Joe says, 'I'd have liked to pick a bit off that turkey myself. I have never been so hungry as the last few days. It's a regular man-o'-war diet now we're on. And us only sporting a pair of cannon. If anyone can get fat on that in four years they must be eating more than their allowance.'

With that remark hanging between them and Joe promising he'd follow him if he could, Charlie makes his way up to the deck, and holds fast to the taff rail on a rolling, pitching sea. Finisterre would be 12 points or more to starboard if he could see her.

Half to himself, he says, 'This'll be the longest time I'll have been away from Mary.'

And lost for a moment in recollections of his last return to Maresfield only a fortnight since, he finds Nicholas Hicks, one of the ship's topmen, at his side. Hicks is a long serving, lairy bastard with a heavy fist and Hold Fast tattooed across his hairy knuckles. So tall, he's always in a stoop below decks, which never helps his mood. But today he's all yellow-toothed smiles.

'Having a breather, Charlie?'

Charlie didn't particularly want company. But they nod to each other, and Hicks says:

'Me too. Here, help yourself.'

Charlie takes the piece of tobacco offered, still moist because they haven't been long at sea, and makes to return the rest but Hicks says with half a wink in his eye:

'No, keep it, I still got plenty.'

They both light up and draw quietly on their cupped pipes for a moment, letting the smoke whip away over the rail. Charlie wonders where this uncommon act of generosity might be headed.

'Wind's doing the work for now, eh?' Hicks looks aloft at the tightly set array of sail carrying the ship southwards. 'Boilers just ticking over nicely?'

'Right enough. Number one's on burn down, we keep the rest good and ready, so we do.'

'Nice warm coals, eh, but not too hot?'

'Aye'. He shifts uncomfortably.

'And weren't the officers hoping for a grand Christmas dinner last night, so I believe? Which saw their turkey all dressed just disappear. Right under cook's nose and never heard of since.'

'It's no good looking at me.'

'Ah, no, but I am, Charlie. Now we know you're a man we can trust.'

'We?'

'We which was hoping to dine on goose tonight.'

Charlie feels an urgent need to get back down below, so he stamps a bit of circulation back into his feet and with a tip to his hat is gone.

It's seven bells. Charlie has damped number one, got the rest of the watch restocking the coal hoppers while he wipes the brass instrumentation, dabs a bit of oil here and there, and logs pressures on the hour. The crew's new amateur brass band is blaring away in the forepeak. Its squeaks and a booming drum accompany the creaks and groans of the ship's sinews as she strains along.

When, and he knew it would come, Charlie hears a footstep behind him. Hicks, stooping, holding a heavy, lidded metal pot.

'Quick. Open up, which one's still warm?'

'Oh bollocks,' Charlie thinks.

Hicks plants the pot on top of the coals. Charlie slams the heavy door to No. 1 boiler and Hicks has slipped up the ladder way and into the night.

But on the hour, every hour, Assistant Engineer Spry will do his rounds, and as Charlie knows, he has two hours left on his shift, two hours' cooking time. Mr Spry, a thoughtful man of sympathies, a Christian, has taken to Charlie somewhat, the leading stoker among the fourteen dustmen in the ship's complement. So, as is his wont, he'll sit with Charlie once everything is checked, and so he does. And there in the close quarters of the boiler room, Spry says,

'All's well, Mister Collings? Won't you share a pipe with me?'

Sitting on the bench by the ladderwell, enjoying the down draft of cool air, Charlie fills his pipe, opens the boiler door, takes a taper to the coals and quickly slams it to. Spry wishes to speak of home a while, for parting from home, he has found, with all its cherished recollections, 'gives rise to melancholy impressions.' And in return, Charlie says a little about his wife, Mary, living with her elderly mother, Ann, over at Reedings Farm by Maresfield. He won't say, though, that she's now staying there after their loss. Hard, indeed, to reciprocate this rare moment of intimacy, for it's not just the distance in rank between them, nor his own sadness kept within, but the emergent aroma of a roasting goose with a little onion in the close confines of the hold, out on a rolling sea that he would now have swallow him up.

In a while, Spry says, pressing hands on his knees, standing to go:

'Aye, such cherished recollections will accompany me on this very long voyage over many seas. No, don't get up.'

And half over his shoulder:

'I'll be back in an hour, mind you, Stoker Collings. There's iron work for you to do, if you remember, the linking rods. You may need a bit more coal in number one.'

'Sir,' a knuckle to his forehead.

Alone now, he's caught between the devil and the deep blue sea. But he pulls open the boiler door. He upends the half cooked, hissing goose and its bubbling sauce onto the bed of whitening embers, throws in two buckets of fresh coals, opens the air vent and slings the pot to the far back of the stokehold. And he leans back in the shadows, watchful, his long spade ready to hand, awaiting Hicks return.

Later that night Joe calls out from his writing room door, 'Charlie, what rhymes with sail?'

'Gale. Or, it being Christmas, ale.'

'Perfect. So I've been working on a wee song to cheer you up. I'm calling it Turkey Bones.' And he goes…

> *'We was five days out from Pompey*
> *And already getting thinner,*
> *When somebody nicked the turkey all dressed*
> *For the officers' Christmas Day dinner.*
> *There was a hell of a hallaballoo*
> *Captain roaring like a gale,*
> *They found Turkey bones and a nice pinch of salt*
> *Tucked away in the topgallant sail.*

'There's more,' says Joe.

'Try singing that to the Captain,' says Charlie.

Willing William

In the cramped issuing room, Charlie speaks with tears in his eyes as Joe leans on his desk, pen at the ready. For Charlie has asked Joe to write a letter to his wife, Mary, for him.

'My dear wife,' he starts. 'Joe, you'd better tell that I'm fine and well first, in case she gets worried.' My dear wife, he continues,

...and I can scarce bear to share this with you. In Chatham dock, it started, we lost a man overboard, coming back late at night and the gangway unlit. Then, on New Year's Day, off Lisbon, we was passing a ship bottom upward, but Captain Nares says it was too rough to send a rescue boat across, and her keel was clean away. She'd been upturned some days, he said. The following morning, we passed through any amount of oranges floating in the water, some fruit schooner wrecked about here lately.
And it set a dark mood among the hands, like a following bird, a shadow moving above and behind us, so when we was first dredging the ocean floor, for their fossils and what not, the packet hove to and our engine just holding it head to wind, the dredge rope snapped with a fearsome crack, we kind of knew it was due. That day, 3,000 fathoms of rope went overboard.
And I think when we lost our young sailor boy, William Stokes, just today off St Thomas we felt that his death, a death, had been coming. This time an iron block holding the dredge rope, and we

*had already paid out 1,700 fathoms, broke away from the deck
and set flight. It struck poor William, concussing him and worse,
for his body lay at a shocking angle. The snap and the scream came
in the same moment, like a whipping you'd witness in the bad old
days.*

*But to see the young lad lying there, still not shaving and just
turned 16. And him one of the most willing to learn, Willing
William, we'd call him. He was picking it all up, anchoring,
getting away, your knots, compassing, and learning care of the
engines off me.*

*I think I was the first to him, and if he was out cold it was a
blessing. I kneeled by him, my blue jacket laid on him, and his
lifeblood staining the deck, and the gentle thrum of the engine and
the crush of the men about us. The Surgeon came running and we
lifted the lad gently onto the stretcher and carried him along to
the Sick Bay. He was insensible the whole time and only lived two
hours.*

*Ah, but when their precious dredge was hauled in at last, you could
see the disappointment on the faces of the scientifics, a sad haul, a
few scraps of coral and a black ooze. So well may it serve them, for
their disappointment seemed greater than our grief.*

*Early evening next day the bell tolled for his funeral and all the
ship's company, and the officers and the scientific gents, attended on
the main deck. We lowered his weighted body into the sea and let
him go. And worse, I had made a promise to the boy's father when
we was all signing on. The boy came up from Deal, his father was a
Channel Pilot. He said to me to take care of the boy.*

*I think I've learned enough to know that grief and pain don't share
well. And I'm telling this to Joe now, in the dark of the day, down
with the engines where I can scarce hold my trembling smoke, and
let the tears run as they will.*

Whip in hand

Charlie blinks in the sunlight as he climbs up to the main deck from the mess room, with a decent wash and a nice clean blouse, a plug of best tobacco tucked in his hat and some pennies in his pocket for the bars of Bahia beckoning. The gangway is creaking and swaying alive at the press of the ship's company for the first shore leave in three months. As he reaches for the rope rails to take his turn ashore, the engineer pulls him to one side, with that apologetic look Charlie has seen before, and before the engineer opens his mouth, Charlie knows what he's going to say:

'Will you stay behind for the getting in the coal?'

'Sir,' he says, and inside, bollocks, bollocks, bollocks.

And there's a little extra fuel to his kindling resentment, because Charlie knows and the engineer does too that they will need a full 200 tons of fresh coal to see them through. For there's no other coaling station along the stretch ahead, from Brazil down through the South Atlantic and on to Tristan da Cuhna and the ice.

Soon a train of coal carts rumbles down the quay, and he's kick-starting the donkey engine to begin hoisting the sacks of coal aboard. But the officer of the watch, this sorry watch, says it's wasting fuel when they can be carrying the sacks aboard. And to a man 'they' are negro slaves, let out for hire by their

28

master. Joe, who knows these things, says they get pennies a day. There's 60 of them getting coal in, and under Charlie's direction, two sacks to a man, they're up and down the gangway and down to the hold, three decks below.

But the hold is full, and 70 tons are still left on the wagons so they must to be stowed up on the main deck. And there's this strong young fellow with a sack upon each shoulder and a fine sweat. As he passes from the walkway to the deck to bring his load on board, one hessian sack breaks open and the whole load, the coal and it must be said plenty of dust, crashes to the deck at the feet of the officer of the watch, all over his fine polished boots for the ambassador's welcoming concert party that afternoon, and on the breeze he's soon all smothered in the finest black.

A harsh blow is struck, and whip in hand, the gang master adds his pennyworth. Charlie fetches a shovel and a spare bag and looks the negro straight in the eye as he hands them over. In his own resentment, for the best of this fine day is passing, Charlie does not himself come between the man and the brutal thrashing, even though, in truth, it does offend him. The more so for this is not a well-liked officer of the watch. No doubt, he reckons, a day's pay will be deducted for this random blow of fortune.

Eventually, the last of the coal is stacked on deck, and the carts on the quay are set to roll away. Charlie takes back the shovel and broom, and while the gangmaster is handing the officer of the watch a chitty to sign, neither of them sees the twist of best Navy Cut in the hat pass from one black hand to another.

Inaccessible Island

OCTOBER 1873

Charlie Collins (centre), Inaccessible Island, October 1873.
Challenger collection, National Maritime Museum, Greenwich.

Three weeks out from Bahia, the young, well-liked Sub-Lieutenant, Lord Campbell, writes from his cabin on the lower deck: 'The old *Challenger* went bowling along under full sail at the rate of ten or eleven knots: but these winds were cold, so cold to us who had been melting only ten days before under a tropical sun.'

A 900-fathom trawl off Tristan Da Cuhna, deep in the South Atlantic, brought up nothing but a whale's ear-bone and bits of pumice. But another plunge to the same depth retrieved 'One or two fish that are probably new, and several of them totally without eyes, but with an odd white patch on top of their head which may act as a sensitive organ in their stead.'

On 15 October 1873, the ship dropped anchor off the towering island of Tristan Da Cuhna. Once ashore, the crew heard various islanders' stories concerning the plight of two stranded German sailors, the Stoltenhoff brothers, put down by their whaler on an island to the west two years ago and no word of them since. Their southbound whaling ship had first called at Da Cuhna to provision, and then left the brothers, voluntarily, it was said, on Inaccessible Island to hunt for seal fur, meat and oil, to be picked up by the whaler on its return. But the ship did not return, foundering in Antarctic waters.

Inaccessible Island lay just beyond the western horizon. The following evening, *Challenger* left Da Cuhna under plain sail, heading in search of the marooned Germans, dredging and taking soundings on the way.

'Four bells, Charlie, wake yourself.'

The engineer prods at the gently swaying hammock, speaking softly into the stoker's ear so as not to disturb the bodies suspended in sleep around him.

'Captain's orders. We'll need a bit of steam, there's hardly a breath of wind. All sail to be furled, you'll know.'

'Sir.'

Charlie swings his legs down to the deck, and passing the handbasins, sloshes a mug of cold water over his head. He prods two of the steam room watch from their slumbers, climbs down to the engine hold, mechanically pulls down the first boiler's door handle, looks in at the low glow of embers, opens an air vent and begins his work.

In an hour, the screws are hungrily churning the sea. In two, he hears the thump and thud and complaints as the men above are roused to quarters. Breakfast in another hour, but meanwhile there's hard biscuit and mug of cocoa sweetened with goat's milk that Joe, the provisioner, places for him at the top of the ladder.

When he takes his break on deck at midday, there's a breath of a breeze getting up, sails unfurling, halyards tumbling to the deck. And as he leans over the side to the sea's sway and heave that she knows so well, he is humming quietly. Draws the cold clean air deep into his lungs. Heads to the stern, and with a 'Thank you' to the goat, pushes a pinch of tobacco through into its cage. To its bleating as he tugs its own beard, he says, 'You're welcome.'

At dusk, the watch observes a light on the port bow, and at orders, while the anchor roars into the sea, sets to burn a blue light to leeward, in reply. The ship waits for the night to pass.

And now the engineer is saying again softly into his ear:

'Do you want this chance, Charlie, to rescue the daft buggers? Lieutenant Campbell wants 10 men for the gig…'

He thinks: 'They'll have been praying for their deliverance.'

Soon, the captain's gig, with ten men at oars, an officer at the helm, a scientist and photographer with his gear wrapped in oils, lands heavily on the hard water. Charlie thanks the Lord it's a calm sea as they pull away to the island.

The day breaks warm, they're all soon at bare chests, with the spray kicking up from the dip and rise of the oars. He's deep in thought, lost in the rhythm of the rowing.

And such an island as now takes shape. Not named Inaccessible on a whim but more like on a prayer, for its cliffs rise sheer from the shore to a thousand feet or more, and scarcely any beach save the narrow strip to which they are headed, with its two tiny figures now emerging from the back of the strand. And there's penguins flapping about them in the low swell, and a screeching swirl and cry of mollymawks and gulls echoing off the cliffs. And he thinks, like a survivor, they'll never have been short of an egg or two.

And away from the engine-room dark of the lower deck, in this light and in the easy rhythm of this work, he thinks again of Mary's last letter, precious few though they are. He returns to the child they lost more than two years since, that October, and them just married a year. How will she be bearing up, Mary, without either of us? Mary, with her auburn hair tied back and her sweet round face half smiling. He'll ask Joe to help with a reply when they're back on board.

But a smooth sea and a fine day make the landing easy. The boat now crunches onto the shingle, and to sustain the momentum the crew leap into the water, five at each side, lifting it forward on the swell and up on to the beach, to the comfort of the officer class and their precious equipment. The Stoltenhoff brothers, with their hardened bare feet, scramble over the rocks, grab the boat to help with the last of the hauling.

'Friedrich, Gustav,' they say, gripping hands and won't let go. They stand in an unspeakable kind of joy, in shredded clothes as ragged and wretched as he's ever seen. They don't pull on boots as do the crew, for they have none.

A waterfall pours over the cliff, and close by is the brothers' hut, the roof and part of the wall thatched with tussock grass, on a foundation of stones from the beach, with a small piggery, long since empty. While he gazes at the pitiful dwelling, Gustav takes his hand.

'Mein Brude. Wilkcommen. Vielen, vielen Danke.'

'You're welcome,' he says, tugging a twist of tobacco out of his hat, for sharing.

While the brothers drag open a rescue bag of clothing, boots, tobacco, the scientist kneels prayerfully at the strandline, rummaging for answers among its mass of driftwood, shells, feathers and old bones, bleached white and pitted like coral, skeletons from the seals the brothers caught, or from whales once stranded.

Inaccessible Island
A rescue recounted

Inaccessible Island

Inaccessible Island,
That rock on the horizon,
Where's two Boys abandoned offshore.
Ain't right, cried the crew,
And to the long boat they flew,
For every sailor's a brother, they swore.

And as they hum and they draw,
And pull together some more,
Charlie's prowling in memory's dark hold.
For they don't see the salt tears,
For his wee son so dear,
Lost away, a mere three months old.

While they draw near the great granite stalk,
A thousand gulls and shrill mollymawks
Rise and dive as the rock bursts alive.
In on the tide they reluctantly pull,
Past the wreck of the Boden Hall,
And those devil birds that would eat out their eyes.

Now riding over black stones,
And bleachin' whales' bones,
They leap into the sea on command.
As he hears their joyful cries,
Upwells a bead in Charlie's eyes,
For two Boys stumbling,
Barefoot tumbling down the strand.

Termination Land

FEBRUARY 1874

Six bells sound of the first watch, the wakeful hour before midnight. In his eight by six, windowless cabin, as Navigating Sub-Lieutenant Herbert Swire rubs his eyes, he realises he's been turning over in his sleep their fruitless quest for Termination Land.

In his diary he wrote before turning in: 'We were at the exact spot the Yankee expedition marked on the Chart as Termination Land, & no sign of land was to be seen; soundings were taken, & the depth was 1,300 fathoms, a certain indication of no land in these high latitudes, for all around Kerguelen & Heard islands the depth was only about 100 fathoms. We steamed for 2 days in all directions, but saw nothing but ice, so may conclude that Termination Land has no existence, & the Yankees were deceived by a large iceberg, or well defined cloud.'

Unthinking, he notes the condition of sea and ship, swings out of his bunk, wets his face, washes away his dreams of charts and fancies and finger combs his blond hair. He lights the oil lamp hanging plumb line steady from the ceiling. Beneath, in its yellow glow, his table eases to and fro. To the creaks and murmurs of timber and crew, Swire opens his diary, to a page anew:

'For one mortal month we have been at sea without one sight of land, Termination or not, and only once were we chancing across a ship. I am sick of it. Very much so. Therefore, when I say we have been sounding and dredging as usual, during the last nearly two years it is a mere description of proceedings. I overhear the men name it the drudge, and so it has become.'

'For my part, I play the fiddle nearly all day, at least when I am not on watch or doing other duties, so that I manage to forget to grumble. He is a most miserable man, who at sea, has not plenty to do. Do something, no matter what, and things rub along.'

He lays down his pen, and as he begins to play *The Minstrel Boy*, laying bow across string, the notes of the old Irish air rise and fall and carry away, leaving a pathway in their wake that will stretch to time's horizon.

> **The Minstrel Boy to the war is gone,**
> **In the ranks of death you will find him,**
> **His father's sword he hath girded on,**
> **And his wild harp slung behind him...**

At seven bells, there's a rap on the door. It's a half hour before he takes the watch. Joe, the assistant steward, provides a hot drink and meat sandwich. *What does he write about?* Joe wonders.

'How time passes,' Swire resumes. And with plenty of that commodity available, he continues:

'We officers are in four watches. Two lieutenants and two subs, so in four days I have to keep seven watches. I may as well explain how the watches go. There are seven watches in every twenty-four hours, eight bells sound in each, and they are named thus:

Morning watch	4 to 8 am
Forenoon	8 to 12 am
Afternoon	12 to 4 pm
First dog	4 to 6 pm
Second dog	6 to 8 pm
First watch	8 to 12 pm
Middle watch	12 to 4 am

Say, as I go as officer of the Afternoon Watch, when the watch ends at 4 p.m., I have nothing further to do until midnight. Being as we are in fours, that means every fourth watch comes to the same fellow.' A small poem almost comes to him:

> *'A sailor to the sea is gone,*
> *On the stormy ocean you will find him,*
> *His mission to sound the deep unknown,*
> *As he grieves the ties ....'*

But he loses the thread.

'This ice work is getting very monotonous. Today broke dark and stormy as I came off watch, but dredging was decided upon, with the stokers at work getting up steam for holding her head to wind. Stoker Collings and two men worked the donkey engine by turns, to assist the men to lower and raise the cables. And all the while, the Philosophers peering over the side when they dared, taking their fob watches in and out of their waistcoats. When the dredge came up towards the middle of the day, what was their chagrin let alone ours to find that it had never reached the bottom. Empty, so it was. By this time the wind was up to a strong gale, no further dredging was to be thought of. We then steamed away towards a moderate sized iceberg, to use as a shelter against the wind and sea.'

'For my part I am thoroughly sick of it, and ready to go north at a moment's notice. It is now two months since we left the Cape, and not having touched at any inhabited land since then, we are beginning to ponder the delights which await us in Australia.'

Swire bites into the stocky sandwich.

'We continue to enjoy the good things of life on board, not having yet been reduced to salt provisions. We have sheep still left, besides any quantity of preserved meat and vegetables, and wine etc, in unlimited quantity. But the men have to live on salt grub.'

'Bluejackets have a great reputation in England for mirth in peace time and bravery in war. They are said to be willing, hearty fellows, honest to a fault, trustworthy. Let us examine these popular delusions. Brave, I will not attempt to disprove. But I fear they are not very honest. Aboard ship, they are only to be driven to their work by inflicting summary punishment upon the skulkers. They are constantly murmuring against those in authority, cannot be trusted in any capacity without an officer to superintend. I think of the turkey, goose and duck that disappear habitually.'

'Were it not for the Marines, they would be quite beyond the control of their officers.'

The same men he despises and loves by turns. And in such a shift of mood, writes on.

'Was it only yesterday? We could not see a hundred yards in any direction. The crow's nest for the masthead man is made out of an old tub, he was straining his eyes and freezing by degrees. The full force of that icy gale was something terrible for the men on yards. And all the rest of us enjoying ourselves down below round the fires, when, 'Clear lower deck' was the sudden cry. Up into the howling storm and driving snow, to find an iceberg looming large and fearful, and the ship surely set for the rugged ice that garnished its base. 'Topmen aloft and loose the topsails!' came the order. And how those men made it to the tops and loosed the frozen sails I don't know, but it took them a very short time, and saved the day. This assisted the screw in forcing the ship astern. The men then came sliding down ropes and scuttling down rigging.

But enough. To tell the truth, my fingers ache. Having thus relieved my mind on this subject, let me make my peace with my brother sailors and endeavour to get on pleasantly with them.'

A moment before eight bells of the first watch, for the timing is in his bones, the boat lurches violently as Swire shoves into sea boots and a thick monkey jacket, pulls a sou'wester over his peaked cap, and pulling on mittens, steps out into the fug and grumble of the messroom on the lower deck. With a salute to the men also readying, leads the ladder climb to the main deck, to greet the dark and gathering storm.

Some hope, some anchor
January 1875

He tells me the cross on his right arm is for hope. Hope and anchor. Well, some hope, some hope. I must be brave enough to face this... this troubled water, troubled water.

The Laundry House, Reedings farm. Mary sits in the lattice bay window of their living room, takes a sip of tea and places the cup back on the saucer on the lap of her broadly spread dress. Twists her wedding ring, as she does every morning at this time.

He's been away now two whole years. Two whole years. Had he not gone abroad, we would be together this New Year's day.
I write to him, but get so little back, and some of them not in his hand. The letters. They come like the seasons, almost. Four a year. Says in his spare time he carves little keepsakes for me, of whale-bone, of soapstone. That can't be all he does.
He's never mentioned the little packages I tucked in his ditty bag the day he left me, for him to discover somewhere. A sprig of lavender for fortune, a twist of sweet tobacco, strong thread for his housewife's pouch.
He wouldn't let me near the ship. Walk me to the station, was all he'd say. Gone in a puff of smoke.
So few letters. Enough weeping to fill a well

*This year, our fifth anniversary. My brother, Henry, will come by
with his smile, asking for news. I'll make him tea.
I so little understood, thought how this life would be. Would it be
easier if I lived in a sailor town?
Said he'd be the best paid of the stokers, there'll be plenty for us
when he's back, finally. And, in the here and now, it's what, raw
hands. So little time to read to the children at the school as I'd like,
and no child of ours, no child of ours there either. Since we lost
poor John Charles.
But this afternoon, my brother Henry and I will walk out a while.*

She gets up from the window. Stands looking at his empty
chair…

…Just as, on the far side of the world, Charlie and Joe take
their seats on the train from Kobi to Osaca. There's half a dozen
Challengers in the compartment, second class but comfortable,
tickets courtesy of the railway company. The line has only been
opened twelve months. The engine drivers and stokers are
Englishmen, with whom Charlie has passed a few moments
before boarding, up on the footplate, thinking these stokers
have it easy with all the breeze and fresh air blowing about.
The carriages are built in Birmingham.

As the train winds round the bay, puffing out steam at four
beats to the bar, he gazes from the window, fingers interlocked
on his lap, passing time, for time he has aplenty, as they sail by
fields of wheat and barley almost ready to cut, fields of wheat
and barley a full season ahead of Reedings Farm.

Sounding 139

23 March 1875

It's been a warm, even sweaty night. Navigating Sub-Lieutenant Herbert Swire, roused from his slumbers a quarter hour before the start of the Morning Watch, has given the sounding crew their orders that they, too, know in their sleep. The sea is flat calm, a following breeze if that, but he has seen to it that all sails were furled. Gone down to the hold for a word and a good morning to Leading Stoker Collings. The steam to be got up for the slowly churning screw must just be enough to hold the vessel head to wind.

The previous day, he had the cable stacked ready by the winch on reels 3,000 fathoms' length, with red, white and blue flags tied at 25, 50 and 100 fathom intervals to mark the length paid out. At his command, the weighted sounding line was winched out over the side to begin its descent into the ocean dark. This must be the one hundred and thirty-ninth sounding station of the voyage, and almost all of them he has led.

It's now six in the morning, the decks freshly holystoned to greet the new day. All hammocks are piped up and stowed, and breakfast is underway of cocoa, biscuit, and bit of cheese if a sailor has his own, and a smoke.

As the line is winched back up, the crew see the scientists are jubilant, and Swire has a grin the width of which the men had never seen.

'Glad he's happy,' Henry Hicks mutters to the next man, who tells him to shut his face. Their job now is to walk and haul, walk and haul the dripping hefty sounding line as it comes back up on the winch. For they've never paid out so much line in one drop. Nor had to haul so much back up.

As the line winds up they detach the three cast iron sinkers, a hundredweight each. Then they carry the rope along the deck, turn it round the capstan at the stern, lay it down and return. The 18 horsepower winch can haul the line up from the depths, just about, but the men have the bulk of the work to do of laying it out to dry along the deck. It's wet to boot, slippery to grip, strung with shining weed and alive with shells and little wriggling creatures in the weft.

'Do we Stormalong, my dears?' someone calls, one of the best of singers among the men. A slight of a song for a sensitive officer, but one to relieve the monotony of the capstan walk. So he gets them going on a fine baritone:

'Oh, poor old Stormy's dead and gone.'

And together they give it back: 'Timee way, you Stormalong.'

And he calls, 'Old Stormy was a good Old Man.'

And they give, 'Aye, aye, aye, Mister Stormalong.'

And so they walk the song through verses and chorus:

We dug his grave with a silver spade,
Timee way, you Stormalong.
His shroud of finest silk was made,
Aye, aye, aye, Mister Stormalong.

We lowered him down with a golden chain,
Timee way, you Stormalong!
Our eyes all dim with more than rain.
Aye, aye, aye, Mister Stormalong!

An able sailor, bold and true,
Timee me way, you Stormalong!
A good old bosun to his crew.
Aye, aye, aye, Mister Stormalong.

I wish I were old Stormy's son,
Timee me way, you Stormalong.
I'd build me a ship of a thousand ton.
Aye, aye, aye, Mister Stormalong.

I'd fill her up with New England rum,
Timee me way, you Stormalong.
And all me shellbacks they'd have some.
Aye, aye, aye, Mister Stormalong.

Now poor Old Stormy's gone to rest,
Timee me way, you Stormalong.
Of all the bosuns he was best,
Aye, aye, aye, Mister Stormalong.
Traditional

Never once in almost one hundred and fifty soundings have they let out this much line. As the sounding rod finally clears the water and hits the landing platform, there's jubilation among the scientifics, for they've never before used more than half of a second reel. They reckon the ocean is some 4,600 fathoms deep to the sea bed, well over five miles.

The sailors lean over the side, having a smoke, glad of a standing breakfast, but the scientists, Swire among them, form a beard-scratching circle. There's some doubt about whether the sounding rope formed a true perpendicular line from the ship to the seabed. There's meant to be a one hundredweight sinker for every thousand fathoms of line released, but only three weights were attached as it was let go.

'Who amongst us knew it would be so deep?' says Wyville Thomson.

'We can attach a fourth sinker, but not a fifth, I fear,' says Swire. And that is agreed, for Swire believes the line will break under the greater strain.

One of the thermometers survived to reveal the water temperature on the sea floor as three degrees Fahrenheit above freezing. The other device imploded under the intense water pressure.

Swire breaks away from the huddle, goes over to the men. 'We'll send it down again, boys. And we'll need another sinker and two more therms.'

'Aye, aye, aye, Mr Stormalong,' says Hicks, under his breath but not quite.

But the line goes overboard again, with four sinkers and two replacement patent thermometers. Hours later, the seemingly boundless deep gives up its secret: the sea floor at this station lies at 4,475 fathoms.

The scientists gather in their wooden cabin on the aft deck, and as Mr Swire steps in to join them, Professor Thomson raises a glass, saying, 'Here's to the greatest reliable depth ever obtained. A deep ocean valley almost as much below the surface of the sea as the peak of Mount Everest above it. To the Swire Deep!' And the scientifics say amen to that. Nor would the men in want of a glass deny the man his day.

Leialoha

27 July 1875

Challenger has moored in smooth waters within the coral reef, close to the Honolulu shore. The captain's much promised shore leave follows countless miles of watery solitude since Japan. The want of a favourable breeze prolonged the voyage, and the expenditure of coal.

But at daybreak, there stood Oahu on the horizon some twenty miles distant, at first a line of grey barren peaks rising out of the quiet sea, then the detail as the ship neared. A line of surf, a line of swaying palms, the imposing headland of Diamond Peak, then Honolulu town itself, hidden among trees, save for the prominent hotels and church spires that rise above the canopy. A great crowd has assembled for their welcome, their cries of 'Aloha' everywhere.

Charlie and his mate, Peter Kane, coal trimmer, works to him, same birthday as it happens, are now sitting at ease on the verandah of the Ship and Whale on dusty Union Street. Each has a yellow garland, a glass of iced lemonade and a piece of lemon cake to hand, for it is a 'dry' Sunday, save for the flask of rum. The shady wooden verandah is smothered with flowering creepers, a well-kept lawn in front, a brilliant array of hibiscus, geraniums, fuchsias and more besides, ranged in front of the wooden balustrade, which Charlie leans over to discreetly rid himself of a coal black spittle.

A troupe of careless, already garlanded bluejackets rides by, in from the plains, kicking up a dust, astride their horses as they would a topsail yard in a breeze, hanging on to hats, manes and saddles.

It's two shillings for an hour's hire. The last horse he rode was a donkey at St Michael's in the Azores. It's customary here, they see from their shady perch, for the women to ride the same as the men, astride of their animal. To see them on this fine afternoon in their white muslim dresses galloping along the streets by scores, with their long black hair streaming behind, and some with a baby in front, is to see a pretty sight, they say. The European ladies ride the same as in England, but where everybody else rides astride, side saddle looks ridiculous.

'What do you fancy?'

'A ride, more than anything,' he answers.

They make their way down to the shore where the main street ends and the yellow sand begins, by neat wooden cabins and grass huts, hidden among palms, bread fruit and banana trees. It's late afternoon, children, even infants running in and out of the surf. Groups of two or three horses stand idly by their owners.

'This one's mine,' he says.

'Horse or the lady by it?'

'Get away,' he says, taking the reins. How do you do this? he thinks.

So the tall woman in a long, coloured loose gown that reaches to her ankles, hair in two long plaits down her back, a crimson garland, holds a horse steady and hands him the reins, smiling.

The horse, though, has looked at him, as if knowing this is a sailor as likely to end up facing the stern as the prow.

Charlie reaches for the coins in his pocket. But she shakes her head, says in fluent English, 'Only when we finish. Come, I'll show you.' She hitches up her dress and barefoot, mounts effortlessly.

Left boot in the starboard stirrup, he hauls himself up into the saddle, finds himself facing forwards. 'You can bugger off, Pete, if you want,' he says.

And they set off, not down the busy main streets athrong with sailors, or out to the plains between the town and the backdrop of red brown peaks, but westward along the beach and away and away from crowds.

On their third day out riding, wind in his beard, they've taken the track up to the encircling crest of Diamond Peak, a long quiescent volcano rising from the shore, and reined their horses down into its fertile bowl, met a milk cart on the way and drank a tinful of milk each. They rest by the wayside while the horses graze.

She tells him her name is Leialoha.

'Means darling child,' she says.

'Oh,' thinking of a once darling child.

She frowns. He says, 'Charlie. My name is Charles. After one of our kings. No, no…'

'King Charles!'

She leads them back up over the rim of the volcano and down to the shore, between palms and sea, and they are just gathering pace when there's a crack as his horse loses a shoe hitting bare rock hidden beneath thin sand, maybe a mile from town.

They must walk back to the main street, and they do so, him saying he's shod many a horse in his time, in Maresfield. To her brother's blacksmith's shop, down the end of a long side street. And as he has done so easily on the other side of the world, Charlie instinctively reaches for the tools, is hammering a new shoe into shape. He hands it to her brother who is holding the mare's hoof ready.

The ship's gun goes at eight, just then. He takes her hand, slipping the bent shoe into his pocket. 'Tomorrow, is it?'

Now Peter Kane joins him in the skiff with half a dozen *Challengers* as they pull the hundred yards out to the ship. And being as he's a fine singer, he's picked up an island song, so he calls *Aloha 'Oe*, and they hum as he sings:

> *Alo ha oway,*
> *Alo ha oway,*
> *Eke ona ona ho*
> *Ekalipo.*
> *One fond embrace*
> *Aho eyah ho,*
> *Until we meet again.*

Amen to that, Charlie thinks. Yet his conscience will hum like a bow string all night.

Homecoming, Chatham

11 JUNE 1876

And fare-the-wheel, my only Luve!
And fare-the-wheel, a while!
And I will come again, my Luve,
Tho' twere ten thousand mile!

'A Red, Red Rose,' Robert Burns.

Mary has walked the mile or more from Chatham Station, down Railway Street and through the crush of Rochester High Street to join the wives, relatives and friends assembling by the Command House entrance to Chatham Docks. A band is thumping away on the other side of the high brick wall. It falls silent. The crowd starts back as two cannon are fired, followed by hurrahs on both sides of the gates.

It's early afternoon. She now sits on a bench a little way back from the dockyard gates, separate from the animated welcoming crowd, in her deep blue, high waisted dress with a high collar, three soft white buttons and a sprig of heather pinned on. Her broad forehead creases slightly as she looks up from her book. For a travelling companion, she has to hand a small, blue-covered edition of Songs from Robert Burns. Has re-read those words she has held onto, *And I will come again, my Luve*. She admits to the recurring thought, *Will I even recognise him, or him me? In truth we have shared so little time together. Our whirlwind marriage...* In her handbag there's his last letter dispatched from Valparaiso, taking three months to arrive.

Dressed in his bluest and whitest number ones, Charlie anxiously searches the crowd, his wages just paid off, all hands granted a week's leave. He thinks, *It's been a long time since I've seen her, three whole years and more. Will she be waiting by the dock now? Or will she be gone?*

And then, pulling free from the back slapping, heaving crowd, he draws quietly alongside her, hoists her gently upwards, swings her inward to his broad chest, and all restraint is discarded between them as their shared tears wet their kisses.

Black Rock, Brighton

AUGUST 1879

And three years later, that would be one late summer Sunday afternoon in 1879, as Charlie is walking in his somewhat rolling sailor's gait along the wave-cut strand east of Brighton, with Mary beside him on his arm, expecting their second child, he looks up at the towering white cliffs of Black Rock, luminescent in the lowering sun, coarse veined with sparkling flint. There comes to his mind those days when the surrounding bergs soared high above the top gallants, with sea ice extending to the horizon.

Into the ice: *HMS Challenger* collection, National Maritime Museum.

A bleached landscape of sea ice and bergy bits now lies before his inward eye, of wind-honed ice boulders, or else high runs of pressure ridges staggering like decayed teeth, or of them blue-white castles slowly overturning into their sea moats.

And out there on the open water, immense numbers of whales spouting wherever you turn, their great carcasses rolling along. A fine crimson sunset followed by a white, silvery twilight in the western sky. And he looks to her and says:

'That's a berg,' pointing up to the chalk cliffs. 'That's what they're like. Imagine the whole sea full of them. And whales. And no sunset. All night long just a bright red line glowing along the horizon, broke here and there by the sharp cut form of a berg. Aye, coal black against the sky there. Black rocks.'

As she squeezes his arm, he decides that, for now, he'll keep to himself destiny's brush with an iceberg, deep in the Southern Ocean.

In on the tide, Brighton

AUGUST 1886

Joe Matkin, civil servant, once a steward aboard the *Challenger*, leans on the promenade railings overlooking Brighton beach. Shading his eyes from the sparkling emerald sea, he watches the men unloading mackerel crates from the boats come in on the tide and winched to the top of the shingle. Tie loosened, and wishing he could at least but remove his waistcoat, Joe sees the

Brighton Fishmarket, *Brighton Maritime Museum.*

57

broad back of a man, the back of a man he couldn't but recognise, even after, what, a decade since they docked at Sheerness?

He looks at his pocket watch. Two hours until he's due to rendezvous with his wife, Agatha, at the Palace Pier.

Soon enough, somehow, not sure how, Joe finds himself once again on the end of an oar, as Charlie has them pulling out for his few lobster pots a mile offshore out from Black Rock. Collar, tie, jacket, waistcoat, shoes and socks are stored away dry in the prow, his trousers rolled to his knees.

'Didn't start off well, did it?' Charlie is saying, as their arms retrieve an easy boat pulling rhythm. 'Losing that poor marine fellow over Sheerness dock, before we even got underway? Storms on the way out, if I'm right. And rowing them very poorly men ashore for the train at Deal.'

'Aye,' Joe says, a little out of breath and condition, sweat already staining the armpits of his white shirt. But he gets the breath to say, 'And then when we did get to Pompey, all the Lords and Ladies the Admiralty could muster come on board. Ordering more wines and pickles for the officers and thinkers, if I rightly recall. A Merry Christmas to the Queen as we passed the Isle of Wight. Then more of that damned weather, knocking us all about, and losing all the mess crockery we paid for out of our own pockets.'

'Crockery be damned,' says Charlie. 'Sea come right down the hatch and on top of the engine, nearly put out all our fires. Without no steam we'd have rolled right over.'

'I was pitched right out of my hammock that night.'

As they reach the first cluster of lobster buoys, they drift on their oars a while, the shouts and cries from the bathers in sun and sea scarcely reaching them.

Joe takes both oars to hold the boat steady, the old aptitude still available to him even if his arms ache like billy-oh. Charlie clambers about, bare chested now, that ship's tattoo ever moving across his breast, reaches well over the side, hauls up the first netted pot. The weighted lines are as short as the sea is shallow even this far out. He pinches each creature by its shell as they claw the air, drops them in a barrel of sea water, puts more chum in the trap and returns it over the side.

They've both been thinking of the unlucky start for the *Challenger's* long voyage, and Joe asks, 'Didn't we lose young William Stokes soon after we started dredging?'

'Aye, we did. A fine young boy, he was. I was stood next to him, when it happened. I went to see his father, you know, when we got back. Lived over Deal way, a Thames pilot. I'd met him when he was bringing young Stokes to be signed on afore the voyage.'

Look after my boy, would you.

'I remember,' says Joe.

They manoeuvre to the next batch of cork floats. More grunting as the heavy baskets are pulled up, examined, returned.

'Cheek of it though,' says Joe. 'Took out all but two of her cannon to make room for their science labs and fine cabins. And then soon as we're off the old man put us on man-o-war rations. And I'm setting out the captain's table for the fine Christmas dinner he's laid on for the scientifics, and didn't their turkey disappear? He was hopping mad.'

'So, who do you think it was?' Charlie says, though he knows the answer. A few bones and a bit of salt hid away up in the 'gallants. And he looks at Joe, considering.

'I'd have helped myself to a bit if could have,' he replies. 'Anyway, Henry Hicks, it was, let's agree on that. What a bloody handful, that man.'

'Speaking of,' Charlie says, and fetches his panikin. He takes out a pot of cockles, a twist of pepper and small bottle of vinegar. He sprinkles them lightly over the seafood and they share this first meal since the mess deck back then.

'Them two German Crusoes we rescued!' Joe says after a mouthful. 'What a caper. No boots had they. Living off, what was it, penguins' eggs and goats.'

'I got that photograph of us all on that island somewhere,' Charlie replies. 'Me, I think Captain Nares was more worried about us wasting coal than saving the poor buggers. That long sea haul south ahead of her. If we sailor boys hadn't kicked up a fuss...'

'Wasn't it after that coaling in Bahia Bay?'

'Aye, Bahia Bay. What a sight. Them whipping the poor bastards getting the coal in.'

'Talking of Crusoes, though,' says Joe, 'remember we found Selkirk's cave on Juan Fernandez, after that endless damned draw across the Pacific? Hundreds of old tars' names carved in the rock, ours too.'

And as they drift, they sense where their words are heading. They are sitting quite still, side by side on the boat's centre board, shoulders barely touching, sea flopping gently against the hull. 'My dear father, though' Joe opens. 'As I came away, I knew by his manner when we said our goodbyes that he seemed to think it was for the last time. I still find it hard to believe he was gone four months before I got a letter to let me know. So much time on hand, leaving us to think and fear.'

And he remembers that long stretch across the Pacific till they reached Valparaiso, nearly a twelve-month since news from home. The mail bag was in, but would there be anything for him?

Valparaiso

Pacific Ocean, vast and wide,
Vast and wide
No sail in sight, sail in sight,
Nor bird's eye,
No word from home until they dock ,
No word from home until they dock,
No word from home until they dock at Valparais-oh.

It's been three long years as sea.
Will you remember me,
Like I remember you?
Will you remember me?

And the men stand restless on the deck,
Restless on deck,
As the purser cuts into the letter sack,
Letter sack,
Names a man for whom the waiting
Names a man for whom the waiting,
Names a man for whom the waiting now is ending.

So that brave and fearless man,
Fearless man
No seaman's task beyond his hand,
Beyond his hand,
Now grips upon on his prize
Now grips upon on his prize,
Now grips upon on his prize to hide the trembling.

With his longed for letter home,
Letter home,
He hurries off, must be alone,
Must be alone,
Alone with words to carry him home,
Alone with words to carry him home,
Alone with words to see him home or ease a longing,
Ease his longing.

Now it would be Charlie's turn. He holds back, but then says: 'Aye. Such news as that don't reach us in good time. I lost my boy John when I was at sea. I only got leave to see him but twice, you know. Our Mary was left to bury the poor wee lad on her own. Three months old, is all he was. I was out on *Penelope*, and never heard in time.' He looks away to the shore.

'It was weeks later I got the letter, weeks later. Think it was then she decided against any more, well, until, you know, my discharge.'

'I must be getting back,' says Joe abruptly, reaching for his pocket watch, which isn't there, it's in his waistcoat.

'What you doing with yourself, then?' says Charlie, as they pull towards the beach.

'Married, four years now. My wife will be waiting for me by the Pier. We have a nice place in Pimlico, handy for work. Civil servant, so I am, in Whitehall.'

'You always was a scribe.'

'And you, apart from a bit of fishing, I mean. This isn't what you do, is it?'

'Well, we sometimes cleans the boat up and rows these lucky summer visitors out a mile or two. "It's a lovely ride out," we say. But it's ironwork for me, for the most part. Blacksmith, my trade in the Navy, as you know. Plenty of work in the town, bellhanging in the churches, gas fitting all the houses that can afford it, fancy railings round the theatres.'

They pull hard to shore for the last fifty yards, so she runs straight up the sea-wet shingle. They leap barefoot over the side, out onto the stones and pull her up out of the water. The sea is drawing away down the beach now, tossing just small change back to the shore.

Joe's feet have gone soft and his comic dance on the pebbles shows it. So, he's put Charlie's sea boots on and trousers rolled, they're winching her up to the top of the beach, running the boat over a line of railway sleepers. Charlie has promised a cup of tea and a place to change in his shed beneath the arches. But he'd better be getting along, says Joe, time is running on. Beside the open air stage erected on the top of the beach, the showgirls in pink spotted dresses and conical hats to match are handing out leaflets for the evening show. And Joe's wife, Agatha, passes by, hurrying along to their meeting point.

She gracefully accepts Charlie's offer of a folding chair, and while he borrows some nice cups and a jug of milk from a beach café, Joe changes back to civilian in the back of the shed.

Brighton - fish sellers.
Courtesy of Brighton Fishing Museum.

He's not met anyone else from the *Challenger* since Sheerness, and now he's looking at his besmocked friend talking to his wife. Big unruly beard still, receding hair, big tough hands, part share in a boat. Skin clean, he must have sweated out that coal dust. All that, left behind.

'You've stopped chewing coal then, I take it, Charlie?'

Soon they say their goodbyes, as they must. Agatha turns to her husband, as they walk in step past the clocktower towards the station, 'I'm glad I got you back. The sea, your friend, never let him go.'

'Bloody fine mackerel'

May 1887

It's two bells of the afternoon. Charlie is sitting alone on a bench outside The Ship Inn on Rochester High Street, where he's holed up in a rented room on the top deck, overlooking the sweep of the Medway river. Glass in hand. The half-empty box of fine mackerel between his boots leaks into the warm pavement. 'Mackerel, bloody fine mackerel' had been his cry up and down the main street. Now, this warm, thirsty Easter Saturday afternoon, he's comfortably in his stride.

'Ah,' says the tall young man, in a tidy, black suit who has maybe come from chapel, who now sits down beside him. 'So here you are. I'll have a couple of those before I go, your very fine mackerel.'

'So you heard me calling.'

'Could hardly miss 'un.'

'Brought them in fresh this morning. People round here seem to know the fishes are in before the boats even gets alongside.'

'They live by the tides. You're not from round here then?'

'Last here in '76, came in at Chatham dock. More than ten years since.'

'How's that then?'

'We was been paid off at the time.'

'So what brings you back here?'

'You're full of questions.'

The young man moves to get up.

'No. No, no, no, stay, young man. I'd had a belly full of the sea at the time, that's all. Thirteen years in service. But it pulls you back, so it does. Like you're on the end of a long line and you don't know the hook's up your arse till it starts reeling you in, reeling you in. See this fine catch, or what's left of it. You'd never find anything to equal what we see'd in the Southern Ocean, such abundance. Fetched up when we was dredging. Of all colours, sizes, blue, gold, striped, banded, some with no eyes in their head, sea horses even, from the tiniest to the greatest.'

'And whales, see them beluga, blowing hard and having such a game amongst themselves. Rolling round the ship like it was a maypole. When we was hove to for dredging.'

'And the ice. Say they bergs down there are white, but they're not. They're blue, or could be purple and big as castles til they turn turtle. Or it can be you'd see our ship's shadow spilling for miles across the ice. And we damn near rammed a berg once but for our shoveling coal fit to burst and we was never so near going down.'

And his words drift away.

'One more pull?' the stranger asks.

'Aye, that's it,' he says, 'one more pull. If you're offering.'

And while the young man refreshes the sailor's glass at the bar of the bare and somewhat gloomy inn, Charlie takes out his pocket book, tobacco pouch and pipe. He could open the pocket book, and were he to do so, there he would find the one and only image he carries of Mary Frances. And he finds that he is sitting very still, won't notice the dew drop gathering on the end of his long nose, and all that he hears seems muffled, distant - the wheel of a gull, the cartwheel clattering by on the cobbles...

'Sir?'

Squeezing the tip of his nose, he takes the offered glass.

'It's what they don't understand, couldn't be expected to, in truth. You're paid off, right enough. You land wealthy. Some as spend it completely away, they're back on the beach and their money's all gone quicker than you can say Jack Sprat. And they're off again on some packet ship. But when I got back we opened ourselves a beer house, the Golden Cross, it was, down Brighton. And then we opened a shop, a bit less temptation, so she thought. And she was right, of course. There was good work, too, smithying in the town. And all's well, you'd think. Then one fine morning you find yourself standing there behind the counter, captain of a bloody shop.'

'Will you return?'

He admits to the thought, 'To sea, did he mean?'

Later that same week, it may be a late afternoon, as Mary leans into a tub of warm water, kneading and pulling at heavy white cotton sheets, she will know without turning that he's standing there behind her. Her soaped hands pause at her task. In a moment she may tremble, but slightly, her head move side to side, but almost imperceptibly. Swallows back her first words, of course, for he might as well have been on the far side of the world, for all she knew.

There cannot but be a reckoning, they both know, for this is the longest of his disappearances. But, for now, she says, 'Will you go up and see to young John for me. I fear he is coming down with a fever. The doctor mentioned diptheria.'

It's gone midnight. Charlie sits holding the boy's hand, places a cool flannel on his forehead. Their John is barely two years' old and struggling for breath. Charlie has been home now three days and he has hardly left his side.

Iron casting, Brighton

19 AUGUST 1901

She whispers, 'Happy birthday, Charles.'

And he takes her warm hand in his, knowing as he rises up from sleep that it's five bells even before the distant toll from St John's will tell him so. She kisses his bristly cheek while she places tea by the bedside.

'Thank you, my dear. What will you do today?'

'Ah, there's laundry, the college laundry. Now, when you get home I dare say there'll be a nice tea waiting for you, so you won't delay, not today, will you?'

And they both know what delay means.

'After tea, Charles, couldn't we take the tram down to the front and have a walk along to the Palace Pier? It'll be a nice evening. Would you like that?'

Their nineteen-year-old, Alfred, is already downstairs at breakfast in their back kitchen, and in half an hour father and apprenticed son will head off together lightly and less lightly to their workshop in Foundry Street. But first, this fresh mid-summer's morning, it being Thursday the 19 August 1901, their four youngest of ages ten, eleven, twelve and thirteen years will, sleepily or otherwise, also whisper their wishes and on his beard land their kisses as he sits with a piece of bread and a bit of bacon before he sets off.

Laundry. There's ten single residential rooms in the Secretarial College just up Ditchling Road from the Level, and Mary's weekly task is to wash, mangle, dry and iron for each student a pair of cotton sheets and pillowcases, plus any incidental washing the college may require. She'd been a laundress before. It's not work she wants, especially now he's found work and it pays well.

But after Charlie had come back from Rochester her father had refused to keep giving her money to cover for his binges. *This is the last time*, he'd said, heartbroken for young John. So the work's undertaken nonetheless, saving for a rainy day, if you like. Her place of work is the single storey extension out the back, with an open range for the boiling water and just enough blowy, sheet-drying space in the yard.

It's a ten-minute walk to the ironsmith's workshop and forge that Charlie rents at Reed's Regent Foundry. And, half a pace behind his father, strides Alfred, thinking:

'How am I going to tell him? Or when? It can't be today. He was out all day yesterday. Yes, it's a good contract that one, yes, a hundred of iron railings and corner posts. For the Court Theatre indeed. Yes. Prestigious work, right to the end of the year, and he'll need me to ...'

'You alright, Alf?'

'Oh fine, Dad, fine. Just a slow starting day.'

He steps into pace beside his father.

Then, he ducks through the workshop door, throws the light switch, hangs up his coat and hat, puts his pipe and panikin on a shelf and hands his father a pair of thick leather gloves and an apron.

Charlie, with an approving nod, turns away as his willing son is already taking bellows to the overnight coals still glowing and, shovel and turn, shovel and turn, throwing coke into the breakfasting furnace…

Coal shoveller, tram driver, coal shoveller, tram driver, coal shoveller…

For the ambitious son, the public tram corporation is advertising for drivers and conductors in the Evening Argus. He's been over to their Lewes Road depot in his good suit, joined the queue, picked up a form, seen that the first services will be running from the seafront come November, and more routes and good wages promised.

But now, with the fire catching well, he slams the door to, opens the air vent, loads two blocks of pig iron into the top ladle sat on the flames. In two hours it'll be ready to pour, so now he crosses the yard to the stores for a barrow of fine moulding sand.

And to Leonard behind the counter, same age as him but you could say happier, he says quietly,

'Can't today, can't tell him today, it's his birthday.'

Feeling his friend's hand on his arm as his father passes by. And Charlie follows back to their workshop a few minutes later, some bits of clean scrap in each hand, saying,

'They was happy enough with these moulds yesterday, Alfred.'

'Well that's good. How many samples do they want pressed?'

'Three railing, two corner bits.'

All being well, a new proud set of railings will embellish the street frontage of the Court Theatre, in New Road, down by the Royal Pavilion. Today, they must finish casting samples to the impresario's bespoke design, for the man requires to see the finished product complete with fancy rosettes and spear-like rail heads before he'll sign on the dotted line.

Together they mix sand, resin and binder, with which they will fill a pair of slim moulding boxes. They level off the sand.

'Get me the railing mould.'

The older man presses precisely half of each hand carved wooden railing into the sand mix. And in half an hour or less the mould hardens off. They prise out the templates.

'There's a little bit in there broken off, where's it from?'

'It's an edge piece, there. I'll glue it back.'

'Nice work, lad.'

They knock the wooden boxes away, lay the finished hardened moulds on the sand-strewn floor, and fit one precisely on top of the other. There's a small opening flute at the end of each mould, one to receive the molten iron, the other to let out any surplus. Alfred places five-pound weights on top of the whole piece to stop it blowing apart.

The metal is ready to pour. Iron sparks dance and fly from the fierce, blood-orange fluid in the crucible, and as Charlie sloughs off impurities with an iron bar, they spill to the floor, sparkling, they vitrify the sand, die. He tips the crucible forward, and with a burst of pure white light in the joy of a great gulp of oxygen the liquid metal spills over the lip and down into a receiving ladle that Alfred is holding steady on its carrying cradle.

And they stretcher the cradle over to the mould, and Charlie tips the long-handled ladle and pours the molten iron into the open flute at one end until they see liquid begin to spill out the other end. They lift away the ladle, and rest.

James Hoyle & Son, Hackney, 2019.

At day's end, passing the Foundry Arms: 'We'll have just the one on the way home, Alfred.'

They take their ale in the shade, for they've selected, cleaned and blackened their best samples for showing tomorrow. At six o'clock and pints later they're kicking off their work boots by the back door, and Charlie is, to be honest, soaking up the pleasure of the renewed best wishes from his family. Shaking hands with his newly-wed son, George, already on the piano in the front room, and stooping to kiss his daughter-in-law, Edith Dapp, who is only a little bit shorter than himself.

And when tea is finished and the iced fruit cake mostly consumed, while they're sat round in their front room, their youngest child, Charlie, says to his father,

'Dad, tell us the one about the turkey.'

'Aye, well,' he sets off, 'we was five days out from Pompey…'

'It was Nicholas Hicks the lairy B!'

And a little later, while George and his wife will see the children off to bed, husband and wife are walking to the tram stop, and Charlie says,

'What would it be, Mary, that Alfred can't tell me on my birthday?'

Loyalty, purity and hope

16 January 1908

As Mary Frances leaves the Open Market by the gate, a wicker bag weighing heavily on her right arm, a woman of some elegance, she notices, steps forward and presses a handbill on her.

'Tomorrow afternoon, can you come, dear? It is a Saturday. Will you support us?'

Come and hear why you should demand your vote, the handbill says.

She returns the woman's gaze, the implications already flicking through her mind. Him away on another of his disappearances, a week so far this time. Ivy next door could mind the children, though she'd be bound to ask where I'm going. The tram fare alone…

'I'm not sure,' she says, thinking of those women evicted from that public meeting in the Dome just last Friday, where a Liberal minister, My Birrell, was speaking, and of the large crowd that gathered over the weekend on the Level, just up from their house in Viaduct Road.

And the next afternoon at 3 pm she finds herself pushing open the heavy oak door to the Ventnor Lecture Hall in Hove. Lines of chairs, some already occupied. Small groups in conversation. Three women, one she now recognises, are setting the top table with a fine array of winter flowering iris and a white blossom she doesn't recognise enclosed in their leaves, and a tricolour banner to match, draping over the front. A cup of tea is offered and declined, and she sits on one side, away from the door, with her bag on her lap. Men, she has noticed, were charged a shilling on entry.

'We welcome all who among you will support our cause,' the host begins, 'And, yes, sir, even those who don't.'

Then a Mrs Pethick-Lawrence is introduced to outline the various reasons why, in her opinion, women should be enfranchised, for ...

'...If women are allowed to vote, the conditions of female workers will surely be bettered. Such questions as no man can hope to settle will be answered satisfactorily. And married women, who at present have no legal claim on their husbands for maintenance, although they play just as important a part in daily work, will be given justice. As things stand, when a woman marries she enters into the service of a master ...'

Derisive laughter, the reporter from the Sussex Gazette scribbles on his notepad...

'Yes, the service of a master who offers her no reward and whom she could never change. For love does not always come and it does not always stay...'

Mary finds that the oration has stilled her breath. She swallows, looking down at her own raw hands.

'Some say the franchise would mean a great amount of dissension between man and wife, but I know of a husband and wife in Australia, no less, who both have the vote but are still very good friends.'

Miss Alice Abadam follows, and in her fine, lilting Welsh accent, is saying,

'This is the great human question of our time, which soars above party... women are breaking down the last of the great monopolies of power, the power of one sex to the exclusion of the other. Women asked for bread and they got a stone, they asked for a fish and they got a serpent, they asked for a vote and they were given their deceased husband's brother.'

And despite himself, the journalist laughs along with the rest of the audience, so that Mary does not hear the door open behind her. 'Budge along,' Ivy, her next door neighbour, says. 'He's back. He don't know we're here.' And squeezes her hand.

Of human bondage, Brighton

JUNE 1918

Mary reaches forward in her armchair for the cup with two aspirins in the saucer. She swallows them with the warm tea, one at a time, and sets the cup and saucer back down on the side table. Easing back, out of the sun this mid-June afternoon, her right arm returns to rest on the white, embroidered antimacassar. Her slim fingers spread gently once more across her inclined forehead. The sound of children's voices plays out somewhere in the back of the house.

Edith Collins, her daughter-in-law, pulls the piano stool away from the piano and perches there for a moment, next to the armchair. Attentive, petite, energetic, Edith is keeping her three children at home in Springfield Road, their only defence while the flu epidemic rages.

Late last evening, while Mary was getting ready for bed, she was overcome by a severe headache and a bout of sickness. Leaving Charlie to care for his wife, Edith put on a coat and hurried the mile to Dr Myskin's surgery. And towards midnight, and calmer now, listening from her bedroom, Mary had overheard them in quiet conversation by the stair, as he was leaving.

'Mother enjoys good health, really, for her age,' Edith had said. 'But recently she's been getting these headaches. They come and go, but this is the first time she has been sick. I'm so glad we have room for them here. And father, too, of course. My husband is away, in the Navy…' Her voice trailing off.

'You did right to call,' Myskin had replied. 'I cannot be sure, but it's unlikely to be the influenza.' Some of her symptoms match, he had said, the headaches, the nausea, but in truth the virus in question was swift and unforgiving in its passing, especially among the young and the elderly. He had closed his bag and turned to go, weary on his feet from a day tending to patients at the Royal Pavilion Military Hospital. 'Call me again, if you need to. The aspirin will help. And rest. She should rest as much as she can.'

Mary had heard the latch go on the front gate.

Now, returning her daughter-in-law's gaze with a small smile, Mary asks, for perhaps the third time that day, 'Has there been any news, dear, from George?'

'We shouldn't expect to hear so soon, mother. He wouldn't say no more than he was heading for Scotland, for North Sea duties.'

'I miss his piano playing,' says Mary.

'Yes, we both do. He can make us smile, though, can't he?' Edith says. Her husband, Acting Engineer George Collins, currently on North Sea patrol with the silent service, keeps copies of his Popular Music Weekly magazine in a pile on top of the piano. The latest broadsheet lies open where he'd left it a week past.

'Here's one of our favourites, the Nora Bayes he played for us,' she says, singing softly,

> *'Sure, you'll get a glimpse of heaven,*
> *Where all Irish hearts belong,*
> *When handsome Jim McCormack sings a song.'*

Mary now sips her tea, the warm sun and medication taking effect. 'You must think I'm a lazy bod,' she says. And as Edith leaves her in peace for a while, Mary returns to her book, *Of Human Bondage*, and reads the closing lines again, depicting a life's course swayed "by what he thought he should do and never by what he wanted with his whole soul to do." Was hers such a life? She shades her eyes, drifts into reflections of her children, one by one. In her mind's eye, as so often, are the three boys she has lost.

First, she will see John Charles, always just a baby, passing away with a last sigh from a fever while they lived over at Reedings Farm. She and Charlie had gone back just last October, taking flowers. A late afternoon sun on the St Bartholomew's square stone tower, a grey-blue sky above. Them now standing back, hand in hand, to look at the small, white headstone, beside the many that seemed to mark much longer lives. The child whom she'd held in her empty arms while her husband was at sea.

'Both our Johns…This won't do,' she says to herself, gets up and goes to the mirror. Looking critically at her face, Mary adjusts the hair band above her high, now lined, forehead and the net holding in place her long auburn hair turning to grey. She wears a high-necked, deep blue dress with sloping shoulders and tight sleeves. She releases the top button, rubs her neck and shoulders.

She cannot get used to this inactivity, yet she struggles to focus well enough to complete the darning and mending of children's clothes she has started.

Mary walks to the high bay window overlooking Springfield Road. Sees again her face reflected in glass. Resuming her train of thought. They are lucky, she knows, to still have their six children to love and to cherish, each established, in their own way, though heaven knows life isn't that simple. And she has placed such value on a proper education, for all of them.

Their Netty, a ward sister at Guys Hospital, in London. Caring for soldiers now at Brighton General. And poor Dr Myskin's there too, he's run off his feet.

Netty, my dear Netty. You have your sister, Nancy, all wrapped round your little finger. And your little Bertie. Why such a quiet boy? Is she unkind to him?

She hears the rumble of the Lewes train on the London Road viaduct. Alfred, independent Alfred. He wouldn't follow in his father's trade. Well, like father like son, I did tell Charles. On the railways, an engine fitter and smitten with religion, what an odd combination. Where that comes from I have no idea. His Elizabeth is more sensible. And their little Albert, another grandson, what a monkey.

A small hand takes hold of hers. 'What are you looking at grandma? You look sad.' Little Stella, a head full of red curls, who will be three years old come 1 July.

'That man over the road, cleaning his windows.' They hear the squeak of a leather rag on glass. The child has been a restless sleeper since her father returned to sea. There's very few people in the town who, in the quiet of early dawn, haven't felt the boom of guns across the Channel. 'Would you like me to read to you now?'

But Stella came to fetch a toy behind the sofa and she's gone in a moment. Later on then, perhaps, Mary thinks.

Mary rests again. Soon, the sound of a horse's hooves clopping slowly up the road somehow worms its way into her afternoon sleep. She's waiting for Charles's homecoming, to Maresfield, to the Laundry House. But he's already found work, somehow he's already at the forge down Maresfield Under Hill, with Harry Edwin, who took it over from his father. He's now wearing a heavy cotton apron, standing in deep shadows at the back of the smithy, behind a blazing red fire of coals. Someone says they have two horses to shoe and get on back to the big house. And her husband is speeding up the Under Hill by the Laundry House window on a bay horse, gathering speed, with another bay in tow, his pigtail blowing back behind him like a tail itself, and he's calling her name...

She wakes with a start to her husband gently touching her warm hand. 'Tea, Mary, tea will be ready soon.'

'Oh, thank you, dear.' She looks up at him. 'Charles, when you came back home, the last time, where on earth did you learn to ride a horse like that?'

My goodness, he thinks. Kneeling stiffly, he looks into her blue eyes. 'Whatever made you think of that, Mary?'

'Well?'

He shrugs. 'They taught us all sorts in the Navy, Mary.'

'And some things they didn't?'

He takes her hand, helps her to stand, though it wasn't strictly necessary. She leans into him, hand resting flat on his broad chest. 'We should go down for tea,' he says.

At around 10 pm, as Mary makes her way upstairs, the pain returns.

'Come, let me bathe your head with warm water,' Edith will say, and in a little while the headache eases. Edith will help her undress and into bed. But a bowl is soon fetched, for the affliction returns, Mary is sick, and sick again. As is often his way, Charles is out for the evening, so Edith calls for her eldest daughter, Edie, to fetch the next door neighbour.

Mrs Tomlinson will help get her back into bed. The vomiting has passed, but Mary is beset by a seizure and will lapse into unconsciousness. Mrs Tomlinson hurries to Dr Myskin's house, but he cannot come out, for some reason, and sends round a bottle of medicine. But they will be quite unable to rouse Mary to administer the medication.

A week later, addressing the Brighton Coroner, Edith says in little more than a whisper, 'And then we lost her, poor dear.' A coroner's jurisdiction was required over this passing, for Mary had died without a medical person present. 'Another doctor was sent for,' she explains, 'but Mrs Collins remained unconscious and passed away at 11.50 pm. Dr May arrived at about midnight, but he could only pronounce her life extinct. It was too late to do anything…'

Pearls before swine

SUMMER 1923

It's mid-evening but Charlie is home early from the Springfield Hotel up the road, where he's been with his drinking cronies. Touching the bent and rusting horseshoe on the window sill as he enters the back kitchen, he growls to anyone listening, before he's even shrugged off his pea jacket, 'They sit there and they talk about dear old Erin, and how much they damn miss it. Well they're a load of bloody hypocrites, they've no intention of returning there. Wild horses wouldn't drag 'em back.'

He leans his cane against the wall and sits by the table where Stella, his granddaughter, she's just eight, is drawing, and she says, 'Who is old Erin, grandad?'

So, he says, 'It's just an old name for Ireland. Where we're from, on my mother's side. It's their home they left years ago, when they were boys, just.'

'Did you leave home when you were a boy just, grandad?'

And he thinks, 'Yes I did. Home, that word home, home. The ship was my home.'

'Was it?' she says.

'Was what, dearie?'

'Was the ship your home?'

'Did I say that?'

And he says, 'I'd only been trying to explain phosphorescence to them. It's like when little creatures in the water glows in the dark when you disturbs them. Like as at night, the first time we saw it, we was heading to St Paul's Rocks we were, and the old bow waves was glowing and sparkling, a blue green light it was as we went ploughing and churning through the sea. There was light enough to read by. It was as if the Milky Way had dropped down on the ocean and we were sailing through it.'

'Or, another time, if we were out in the skiff at dusk, pulling through the waters of some harbour, or along some shore, the oars would drip showers of stars, so they would. Or, sometimes if a dolphin, or a shark, or maybe a porpoise shoots up out the water, swimming around you, they would look like they were sheathed in gold. They streak through the black water like lightning strikes. It's only when they are disturbed do these tiny sea organisms give forth their lights. It's the only light there is down in the deeps of the ocean.'

He pauses. 'Pearls before swine. Talking to them hypocrites in the pub is like laying pearls before swine.'

His granddaughter looks sad for him, takes his hand.

'Would you like your cocoa now?'

'No, I'll get it dear, you go on up. I'll come up in a minute.'

In a while, he's sitting there by her bed, with a little extra something in his cocoa, holding her little hand in his rough paw. The rule is, if she says a word, he has to tell a story about it. So, she says, Cocoa.

'Oh dear me, cocoa. Now don't get me started on cocoa. We had a goat called Cocoa sail with us once…'

'Goat on a boat,' she giggles.

'We had more than that, more like a farm afloat. When we set off last time they had a chicken run like your mum's, except it's on deck, and that was next to the goat's pen. I'd give her a bit of baccy as I went by, and stroke her beard for luck. Next door to Cocoa, because she was brown with a white beard, was a turkey in his coop, and next door to him was the geese running about with the ducks. And none of 'em was a good sailor. Like if a bit of sea came pouring along the deck they'd kick up a right fuss, day or night.'

'I think that boat sailed on cocoa, blooming cocoa. It was up hammocks at four bells, then breakfast at six bells, you see, with cocoa and a bit of hard biscuit. And when I say cocoa, I don't mean like your mum makes, all milky and sweet, and when I say biscuit, I don't mean a nice tasty McVities like Mrs Pettit will sell you. The cook's biscuit you couldn't knock a nail through. If you didn't dunk it, you couldn't eat it.'

'Nope, the grub wasn't up to much, 'less we managed to hook a fish when we was at anchor someplace. Salt pork and pea soup one day, and salt beef the next when we was underway. What they call a man o' war diet, it was, nothing fancy and Christmas coming. Where was I? That last one out, oh dear, we was getting hungrier by the day, and them officers and men of science all on fine dining. Then someone sneaked into the kitchen when cook's back was turned and nicked the turkey…'

But she was asleep.

'My pretties'

SPRING 1925

The young Collins family is returning from a visit to relatives in Dalston, Hackney. Arriving at Brighton railway station, Edith May and her two youngest, George and Stella, change platforms for the Lewes-bound train. Their final stop, London Road station, is just a two-minute ride across the towering viaduct over the main London road. From the carriage windows this fine spring afternoon under a luminescent blue sky the children press noses against glass for a glimpse of the sparkling sea.

There are four shops halfway up Springfield Road, numbers 148 to 154. Number 148, on the corner, is Mrs Oakley's the grocer's. Next door at number 150 is The Cabin, a sweetshop run by Miss Gander. It's overrun by mice. 'Don't buy anything unless it's wrapped,' say people who know. Miss Gander's brother has a Saturday job delivering meat on his bike for Mr Fitt, the butcher's next door. And 154 is Mrs Pettit's the greengrocer's. Opposite this fine parade stands the Springfield Hotel, on the stub of a road leading to London Road station.

First calling into Mrs Pettit's, Edith fetches a few things for their tea: milk, six eggs, bread, spring greens. Then stops by the butchers next door for half a dozen chops, and is walking down Springfield Road to their house, number 47, with her children in tow.

'…57, 55, 53, 51, Mrs Jones, and 47!'

'Hold my bag now, poppet, while I get the keys.'

'47, Mrs Jones, 43, 41…'

And as her mother, Edith May, is turning out her shoulder bag on the top step, Stella jumps from foot to foot, counting house numbers, her red hair swinging from side to side. At ten she's nearly as tall as her mother and as slim and wide-eyed.

Her older brother, George, stands there with his hands in his shorts probably thinking of the steam locomotive that brought them back from Victoria Station, the smoke and ashes piling past the open carriage window.

And, thinking of being back sharing his bedroom with his grandfather, who smokes, smokes, smokes, he asks as they push their way into the cool hallway:

'Is he always going to be living with us?'

'Well, he'll be out now, so go on up you two and put your things away. Bring down anything that needs washing.'

Home now from their three-day family visit to her brother in Dalston, she sits at the kitchen table with a cup of tea and a cigarette. And Stella's soon there, the younger of her two girls.

'Will cousin Charlie really get what for, Mummy, do you think?'

'Well, put it this way, dear. We were having a very nice time. And yesterday, his mother said you could go and play by the flats and not go far, and he took you all the way over to Victoria Park…'

'But it was so hot Mummy…'

'…instead, and you went in paddling in the lake in bare feet, and his boots went missing. His only pair of boots.

'It wasn't his fault.'

'But it happened. They don't have much. It's a hard lesson for him.'

'He had to walk home in his bare feet.'

'That's what I mean.'

'They live at number one, don't they? What does it mean, The Lewis Trust flats?'

'Now if you'll excuse me young lady, I'm making our tea. Pop will be home soon. You two go and feed the hens and put them away, then you can go out front and play till I call you in.'

Birds fed, the two run across the road and up the hill. It's a warm August Saturday, early evening now, with plenty of front doors and sash windows open to the sea breeze cooling the Victorian villas lining the road.

Two small heads peer round the pub door. A low rumble of conversation spills out from The Springfield, where the air is as heavy as the smokers can make it, bears a sweet smell of spilt beer. Their grandfather catches them in the corner of his hazel eye, of course he does. He reaches forward to put down his glass, revealing the crucifix on his right arm, gets stiffly to his feet, hands on hips for a moment, and eases past his cronies.

And, the devoted grandfather in front of his pals, says, 'Hello, my pretties, hello my pretties.'

'Grandad, grandad, can we have some lemonade?'

He pays for two tumblers with a wink to the publican and, pushing open the double doors to the street, he says lowly, 'Here's your lemonade. Now bugger off.'

A laundress, like her mother

7 JUNE 1928

Stella takes Prince for his early morning run round Preston Park then, reaching home, she skips down the sideway of number 47, pulling back on the labrador's lead. He's heading for breakfast, it's her twelfth birthday.

'Here, Prinny,' she calls, serving out two ladles of Mr Fitt's minced and boiled meat scraps. She slips a single hard runner bean into the mix before she puts the tin bowl outside the back door.

Edith, her mother, plants a kiss on her daughter's warm, red-haired and curly top. 'We're all going to help Grandad move today,' she says. 'We'll get his things over to your Aunt Annie's this morning. They can look after him better there, and he'll have a view of the sea. He'll come back for your birthday tea, and no doubt want a last evening with his pals up the road, that we can be sure of. Your dad can run him back to Atlingworth Street later.'

Prince looks up from his breakfast bowl, one eye cocked, mouth turned down, the runner bean marooned in the centre of the dish licked clean.

'Oh, Prinny.' She teases his nose with a kiss.

Her mother, clearing away the breakfast things, says, 'Early on, you know, when your Nana was alive, your grandad plumbed in our hot water, soon after they moved in with us. You were only tiny. You won't remember. We were one of the first in the street. The vicar used to come round for his weekly bath, until...'

'...he chased the vicar away with an axe!'

'Oh yes, he did, well almost. Grandad somehow heard that the vicar was wanting his own hot water in the vicarage, like we had. But Grandad also heard that the vicar had asked someone else to do the work. Charlie was out the back chopping wood, or so he said, when the knock came on the door. The usual time of a Friday evening, so the vicar could be all fresh for his weekend sermons. Charlie answered the door, of course, axe in hand, and some very strong words were said. By the time I got down the vicar was heading quick back up the path. I wouldn't say running, but we didn't see a lot of him for a while.'

'Will you go up and see how your grandad is getting on with his packing?' she says. Charlie shares the front room at the top with her brother, George.

'What happened to Nana?'

Edith squeezes the cloth into the sink, wipes her hands on her apron, leans against the kitchen counter.

"Dear Mary. We were very close you know. Her family was from over Portslade way. She had a lot to put up with, that's no secret. Grandad was away at sea for many years. She enjoyed good health, really, for her age, but she'd been getting these headaches. I think she may have not let us know how bad they were. She had some kind of a stroke, I believe, and the doctors came too late to be able to help her, poor thing.'

'I do remember her a little bit.'

'You were only tiny. She was very intelligent, you know. When Grandad would go off somewhere, she used to take in washing, she was a laundress, like her mother. Do you know, she had a mangle and a horse and cart to fetch and deliver laundry. She sent all her children to a fee-paying school down the bottom of Ditchling Road, to give them a better start, she'd say. She bought your Pop a piano and paid for his lessons. He was playing the piano when I first met him.'

'Pop still does!"

'He should be back shortly. He's over at Patcham, working on the garage. Then we can all wish you happy birthday properly. Now run up and see how your grandad is getting on. He may have something for you.'

Four plumed horses

Replacing the telephone on its receiver, the editor of the newly launched Sussex Daily News leans back in his chair, pinches his lower lip, swivels round and raps on the glass partition, beckoning the newsroom's young staff writer to him.

'What you got on tomorrow?'

'The Brighton races story, I'm talking to…'

'Well you're not. I've just had a phone call from…' glancing down, 'a Mr Ellis Banfield. He tells me that the Royal Navy has decided to honour the passing of a very elderly gentleman sailor known as Mr Charles Collins, a lifelong friend, so he sayeth, late of this parish. HMS *Challenger* was his ship. Famous at the time. A citizen to be remembered. You can cover it. Funeral's tomorrow 3 o'clock. And take Jamieson with you, get a nice picture for the back page. Off you go,' he says, tearing the page from his notepad. 'If you ain't heard of the ship, get down to the Library.'

The editor hitches up his silver sleeve garters and returns to today's copy.

Without looking up. 'And Smithson, don't go no further with that razor gang malarkey. Leave it to the nationals.'

Ambitious Angus Smithson, 23 years old. Back at his desk, his head drops momentarily, then he pulls the script from the Remington and screws it into a ball. 'Hatches, matches, bloody dispatches,' he half says to himself. But he is thorough and will do his homework before meeting Ellis Banfield, the deceased's lifelong friend, in the Bath Arms in the Lanes. From which conversation he gleans by the end of the evening that magnificent were the scientific achievements of the ship, but many were the desertions among the crew. 'The work was too hard and the sea time so long,' Mr Banfield's pal had often said. And the journalist knows his editor's bent well enough to rephrase such revelations as 'It was hard pioneer work from first to last.'

On the following day at the due hour, notebook in hand, Smithson is moving among the mourners as they file out from the chapel, eliciting with a sympathy here and a deft question there the finer details of a life to be remembered. Mrs Annie Hale, one of his daughters, tells him that she was by his side that last evening, when he passed away, of failing memory and taken with a stroke. Another mourner will say that thanks to Mr Collins, there's many a bell hung in the town or a fine set of railings installed. And the journalist turns to see Mr Banfield conversing with a young man with slick black hair, long overcoat, fur collar. As Smithson catches the stranger's dead-eyed look, the man slowly runs his right index finger down the side of his cheek. Then a black sedan pulls up. He gets in the back. It motors away. He writes down the number plate. His hand is trembling.

But the bearers are shouldering the sailor's coffin, and the reporters must quickly position themselves below the road for the memorable photograph. Behind the union-jack draped coffin, the family processes slowly towards Charlie's final resting place, high on the hillside of the west-facing cemetery, forever overlooking the English Channel, and is laid to rest beside his wife, Mary.

And Angus Smithson filed his report for Sussex Daily News of 4 October 1932:

An expedition recalled – Funeral of last survivor, Mr Charles Collins of Brighton

Believed to be the last survivor of the Nares Thomson scientific expedition HMS Challenger in 1872, Mr Charles Collins of 7 Atlingworth Street, Brighton, was laid to rest in the Brighton Borough Cemetery yesterday afternoon.

Mr Collins joined the navy when a lad of 14 and retired at the termination of the great expedition in 1876. The expedition, which was organised by the government, was one of the most gigantic undertakings of its kind. Its purpose was to gain information concerning chemical, bacteriological and biological research work in the great oceans, also soundings of the seabed, depths of the oceans and ocean currents. It was grim pioneer work from first to last.

The Challenger left England in November 1872 and returned in May 1876. The total distance travelled was 68,764 miles and the total time away was three years and 167 days. Many of the leading professionals of the day were on board, and those in command were Captain GS Nares and Captain FT Thomson.

Mr Collins, as a member of the crew on board, had a lot to do with the care of the engines. On his retirement from the navy he came to live in Brighton and started a business in Viaduct Road. He was for many years employed by Messrs. JJG Sanders & Sons Builders of Brighton. When he left the firm, he retired and lived with his sons and daughters for some years. He was responsible for the iron-work of the Old Court Theatre in New Road and other buildings in Brighton.

Mr Collins passed away just past five bells in the evening watch of 29 September. He was in his 85th year.

The funeral, which was private and without mourning, was attended by the relatives of Mr Collins and one friend. The service was held at St Mary's Church and was conducted by the vicar and reverend George C Smith. Father Bates of St Martin's Church was also at the cemetery.

The mourners were Charles, George and Alfred (sons), Edith, Annie and Elizabeth (daughters), Edie, George, Bert, Stella Dorothy and Stella Phyllis (grandchildren), Mrs Purdy, Mrs Amrey and Mrs Chappell (sisters), Rhoda and Elizabeth (daughters-in-law), Mr S Chappell (brother-in-law), Mr Ellis Banfield (a very old friend), and many others.

My mother, Stella Collins, then 17, remembered the day. 'There was a grand funeral through the town, with the union jack draped on the coffin, for he was one of the last surviving members of the *Challenger* crew. Your uncle George wore a short stove pipe hat, which kept falling down over his eyes, only his nose stopped his face from disappearing altogether into this shiny black tube. We children were laughing when we really should have been sober, riding along in a horse-drawn open carriage with the rest of the family. The four black horses pulling the hearse wore plumes.'

Author's Note
Sea shanties

It seemed appropriate to include traditional sea shanties in this story, to which I have added some songs of my own. Whatever tale they tell or conceal, shanties are rhythmic work songs. Some go back many hundreds of years, with their roots in slaves' songs on cotton plantations, and the songs of river boatmen and sailors on fishing, whaling or tall merchant ships.

Often led by a solo singer, the shantyman, they were call-and-response songs to make the crew's efforts more effective by working together. Capstan shanties were carried along by the tramping rhythm of turning round a capstan to raise an anchor or pump water from the hold. Halyard shanties were marked by the hauling rhythms on the yards (ropes) to raise or lower a sail.

In this and the following chapters I have quoted from:

Shallow Brown: According to Stan Hugill's *Shanties from the Seven Seas* (1961), the traditional song started life as a pumping song, possibly of West Indian origin.

Stormalong: Stan Hugill traces the origins of this windlass or pumping song to African-American folk songs of the 1830s and '40s.

Aloha 'Oe (Farewell to Thee), a Hawaiian popular song (1878) was written by Lili 'uokalani, then Princess of the Hawaiian Kingdom.

Mollymawk, or Down Upon the Southern Ocean Sailing, by Bob Watson.

A Song for the *Challenger's* Crew: the writer of this song, mailed to the *Challenger's* crew, is unknown. The song was recorded in 2003 by shanty singers The Boarding Party.

Turkey Bones (2019) lyrics by the author, with arrangements by Maggie Boyd and Jane Perrott.

Valparaiso (2020) lyrics and melody by the author with Nony Ardill, arrangement by Benni Lees-MacPherson.

Silvertown: musical arrangement by Ruth Renfrew, lyrics by Philip Pearson. The London Sea Shanty Collective commemorated the strike with this song as part of the 2020 Totally Thames Festival.

- Part Two -

The Challenger Expedition
(1872-1876)

Ship's company referred to in this narrative

Officers
First Captain of Challenger: George S. Nares
Replacement Captain: Frank Thurle Thomson
Engineering Sub-Lieutenant: William Spry
Sub-Lieutenant: Lord George Campbell
Navigating Sub-Lieutenant: Herbert Swire

Crew
Leading Stoker: Charles Collings
Assistant Steward: Joseph Matkin
Leadsman: Edward Winton
Boy Sailor: William Stokes
Boatswain: Thomas Cox

Scientists
Chief scientist: Professor Charles Wyville Thomson,
Naturalist: Henry Nottidge Moseley
Oceanographer: John Murray
Chemist: John Young Buchanan
Naturalist: Dr Rudolf von Willemoes-Suhm
Artist: John James Wild

1

All the Great Ocean Basins

On 21 December 1872, when all was pronounced ready, HMS *Challenger* set sail from Portsmouth harbour on the most ambitious scientific voyage of the Victorian era. The former man-o-war was now a floating laboratory. The Royal Society, the peerless scientific academy of its time, had persuaded the Admiralty to provide the ship and Gladstone's government the funding for an expedition 'of great importance to Science and Navigation for the Examination of the Physical Conditions of the Deep Sea throughout all the Great Oceanic Basins, and for other special objects therein named.'

The Royal Society's commitment was driven by the ambition of three of its leading members, Professor Wyville Thomson, the influential head of natural history at Edinburgh University; William Carpenter, marine zoologist and physiologist; and Thomas Henry Huxley, anthropologist and one of the Royal Society's Vice-Presidents. Carpenter and Thomson had recently returned from a series of short cruises from the Faeroes to Gibraltar in HMS *Lightning* and HMS *Porcupine*. Using new sounding techniques, the intriguing information the pair had gathered on sea temperatures and on species unexpectedly retrieved from the deep led Thomson to conclude that 'a large proportion of the forms living at great depths belong to species unknown. A new field of boundless extent is open to the naturalist. Many of these deep sea animals are identified with fossils believed to be extinct.'

Carpenter was fearful that Britain's lead in marine sciences would be eclipsed by cruises planned by the United States and Germany. The society moved quickly to appoint Professor Thomson to lead the six-strong team of naturalists, physicists, chemists and artists, all prominent in their respective fields: John Buchanan (chemist); Henry Moseley, William Stirling and John Murray (naturalists); and James Wild (artist). The eminent navy surveyor, Captain George Nares, was given command of the expedition.

The Royal Society set out its instructions to Professor Thomson and Captain Nares in a 20-page memorandum with a recommended route of sail and detailed instructions on the information to be recorded at ocean sounding stations and at stopping points on the way. A spirit of co-operation between sailors and scientists was vital, as was made clear in the captain's brief:

'The objects of the expedition are manifold; some of them will come under the entire supervision of Professor Thomson and his staff, others will depend for their success on the joint co-operation of the naval and civil elements. Many will demand the undivided attention of yourself and your officers; it is not, however, too much to say that upon the harmonious working and hearty co-operation of all must depend the result of the expedition as a whole.'

The expedition was set four main areas of enquiry. 'The main object of the voyage,' the memorandum states, 'is to investigate the physical conditions of the deep sea throughout the three great ocean basins, that is, to ascertain their depth, temperature, circulation, &c., to examine the physical and chemical characters of their deposits, and to determine the distribution of organic life throughout the areas traversed, at the surface, at intermediate depths, and especially at the deep ocean bottoms.'

The naturalists were instructed to 'make complete collections of the plants of all interesting localities, and especially of the individual islands of oceanic groups. Of many that lie not far from the usual tracks of ships, absolutely nothing is known...special interest attaches to their Zoology, Botany, and Ethnology.'

'Secondary, but by no means unimportant objects, are the hydrographical examination of all the unknown or partially explored regions which you may visit, a diligent search for all doubtful dangers which may be in or near your track, with a view to expunging them from the charts or definitely determining their positions, [thereby] compiling practical information of the greatest importance to seamen.' However, Captain Nares was cautioned of the dangers of lingering in the neighbourhood of the Great Antarctic Ice Barrier in 'a single unfortified ship.'

The Admiralty had a further strategic objective. 'Independently of the great scientific interest which attaches to these experiments, it is to be remembered that the rapidly progressing establishment of electric communication between all parts of the earth renders it most important that the accurate depths of the ocean and the character and temperature of its bed should be known. You are therefore furnished with a series of charts on which are shown the spots where soundings are most required, and which, wherever they lie within or near to your course, you will endeavour to obtain.'

And finally, in the instructions to study 'native races,' a single paragraph says: 'Every opportunity should be taken of obtaining photographs of native races to one scale; and of making such observations as are practicable with regard to their physical characteristics, language, habits, implements, and antiquities. It would be advisable that specimens of hair of unmixed races should in all cases be obtained.' This crude objectification of fellow human beings perceived to be of another 'race,' implying that they, too, were specimens of 'great scientific interest,' was not unusual at the time in Imperial Britain, almost forty years after the Slavery Abolition Act 1833.

Testing Darwin

Personal scientific interests influenced the expedition's objectives. For the Darwinist Professor Wyville Thomson, at stake was the quest for living proof of the still controversial theory of evolution. Darwin's *Origin of the Species*, published just 13 years before *Challenger* set sail, theorised that animal and plant species evolved through natural selection. The descendants of marine organisms found today in fossil-bearing rocks on land, the so-called 'missing links,' would be found alive and well in the ocean depths.

Thomson was also going to seize the opportunity to debunk one of the strangest notions of mid-19th century ocean science: that no life could exist below an arbitrary depth of 300 fathoms, an 'azoic' abyss. Furthermore, the expedition would allow him to build on the evidence he gathered in home waters of the circulation and warming influence 'of the great current which we call the Gulf Stream.' He could now explore the great oceanic movements in other seas.

In the aftermath of abolition, Victorians held fast to the belief in European racial superiority: all that was needed was the 'proof.' In 1871, a year before *Challenger* set sail, Darwin had published *The Descent of Man*, sweeping away religious creation myths and instead framing human species as having shared origins. On a personal level, this mattered to Darwin: his family included influential abolitionists. He himself had seen the brutality of slavery first hand on his travels. He rejected the idea that races had been separately created, yet remained ambivalent on the question of whether black Africans and Australians were strictly equal to white Europeans on the evolutionary scale.

For Thomas Henry Huxley, eminent biologist, anthropologist and champion of the expedition as the Royal Society's Vice-President, observing 'native races' for their physical characteristics, language, habits and implements was central to his work seeking to establish what he perceived to be 'a hierarchy of civilisation.' In 1865, in his essay on *Emancipation – Black and White*, Huxley argued that 'no rational man, cognisant of the facts, believes that the average negro is the equal, still less the superior, of the average white man.' It was inconceivable, he argued that if 'our prognathous (ie big jawed) relative has a fair field and no favour, he will be able to compete successfully with his bigger-brained and smaller-jawed rival.'

An advocate of the emancipation of slaves, he nevertheless believed and set out to 'prove' that 'the highest places in the hierarchy of civilisation will assuredly not be within the reach of our dusky cousins, though it is by no means necessary that they should be restricted to the lowest.' Moreover, fulfilling a moral duty to free slaves would achieve a 'double emancipation, and the master will benefit by freedom more than the freed-man.' He would have nothing to fear, for negroes would not be able to compete successfully with his 'superior' rival.

The evidence lay in the skulls, he maintained. After ancient human remains, subsequently labelled Neanderthal, were identified in Germany's Neander valley in 1856, direct comparisons were soon made with indigenous Australians. Huxley described the skulls of Aborigines as being 'wonderfully near' those of the 'degraded type of the Neanderthal.'

In her book, *Superior: the Return of Race Science*, Angela Saini argues this presumption was 'an error at the birth of modern science,' in fatal combination with the imperialist politics of the day. The Royal Society's open brief to its scientists left more than enough room for imperialist ideology to intermix with the stereotyping race pseudo-science of the era.

The Victorian conviction of the relative superiority of Europeans pervades the diaries and notebooks of the *Challenger's* scientists as well as its officers and such an observant crewman as Joe Matkin. Peoples whom they encountered who did not live, look, work, pray or dress like Europeans, they presumed had yet to realise their full potential as human beings. This ideology runs as powerfully as an ocean current through their accounts of encounters with foreign peoples, and in their purchase or unashamed appropriation of ancestral skulls, skeletons, weapons and devotional pieces. The scientists brought home nearly 150 skulls and countless bones for forensic examination.

Meanwhile, the *Challenger* expedition also had a hard-headed geo-political purpose for the British government. Obtaining accurate profiles of the ocean floor was essential for laying undersea telegraph cables - an expanding 'Victorian internet' - from London to Europe, to the Empire and its colonies, and to the Americas. The first transatlantic cable was laid down in 1859. The Admiralty's Hydrographic Office prided itself in producing the world's finest maritime charts. But now the office was being asked questions by the submarine telegraph companies that it was unable to answer because it had not mapped the sea-bed in any detail. This was not a comfortable situation.

As the Assistant Chief Engineer, William Spry, wrote in his account of the voyage, 'There can be no doubt that the invention of ocean telegraphy first stimulated the great desire as well as the necessity for knowledge of the contour of the bed of the ocean.'

Silvertown

The laying down of rubber-encased copper cabling across the ocean floor, massively subsidised by the Exchequer, spurred the growth of new industries along the Thames. Much of the cabling for the electrified telegraph network was manufactured at Samuel Silver's India-Rubber, Gutta-Percha & Telegraph Works in East London. Silver's huge factory was sandwiched between the Thames and the Victoria and Albert Docks, employing some 3000 men and women, with casuals hired during periods of peak demand. The raw gutta-percha rubber, imported from colonial plantations, landed at the company's wharves for processing in its blast furnaces and metal smelters.

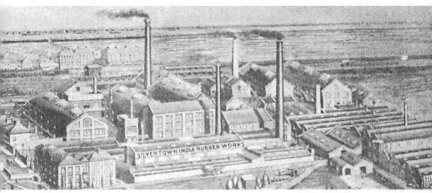

Silvertown India Rubber and Telegraphic Cable Works, London, 1880.

By the late nineteenth-century, the firm, now immensely wealthy, had manufactured and laid one-third of the world's 200,000 miles of submarine telegraph cables. Silver's own fleet of four vessels left the company's wharves to lay the cables on the sea floor. The firm's shares regularly returned a ten per cent yearly dividend.

Yet, as a study by John Tully reveals, the workforce was 'ill-fed, ill-paid, ill-housed, and ill-used.' For the thousands Silver employed, factory hours were grindingly long, hard and insecure. For a few pence an hour, they worked in poisonous mixtures of rubber, sulphur and benzine, melted in blast furnace heat. In September 1889, spurred on by the recent match girls and dockers' tanner strikes, the workers began a four-month strike, part of the growing formation of new unions for the general worker. Their protest upended the London industrial district which bore their employer's name: Silvertown. And from it sprung new unions for working men and women, including the first women's branch of the new National Union of Gasworkers and General Labourers. As Eleanor Marx roused the 10,000-strong gathering in Victoria Park on 6 October 1889, 'The dock strike taught us a lesson. Skilled and unskilled labour must work together. And we can only win by men and women working in combination.'

The London Sea Shanty Collective commemorated the strike in its song, Silvertown, as part of the 2020 Totally Thames Festival. The chorus runs:

> *We're marching down to Silver Town,*
> *Early in the morning.*
> *We'll shut old Silver's factory down,*
> *A new day is dawning.*

But the firm refused to accede to any of the union's demands.

By sail and steam

So it was that with business, scientific and public interest running high, the Royal Society of London was able to persuade the Admiralty to organise and pay for the most comprehensive oceanographic expedition ever undertaken. With a four-year voyage in prospect, *Challenger* was selected for the task, undergoing a major refit at Sheerness dock. She was a three-masted, steam-assisted corvette, 200 feet long with three decks and weighing 2,300 tons. Its four boilers powered a 1,234 horse power steam engine. All but two of her 22 cannon were lifted away to make room for state of the art laboratories, workshops and accommodation for the team of six scientists. A dredging platform was built above the main deck (see page 121).

The top or main deck housed cabins for the captain and senior officers, a vast cooking range, the sick bay, and a purpose built work room built for the scientists. A hatchway led to the lower deck, with cabins for junior officers, and messes and hammock space for the ship's 230-strong crew, including 21 officers, 136 seamen, 50 boys and 21 marines to keep good order. A second hatchway led down to the hold below, my great grandfather's place of work. It held the stokehole for 150 tons of coal, four boilers, the engine room, the steel axle across the width of the ship and the propeller shaft running its length. Charlie Collings was one of the four leading stokers in the steam department, under the command of the chief engineer and including five assistant engineers and artificers, and fourteen stokers and coal trimmers. The hold also provided storage for provisions and the great coils of tar-soaked dredging rope the men would lower to the sea floor.

For wind power, she carried over 16,000 square feet of sails, twenty sheets in all, hung in arrays from the yards of her fore, main and mizzen masts, the jib at the prow and the spanker by the stern. To use the sails drawing power to the full, they all had to be set by the sailors, whatever the weather. At the officer's command, the men climbed barefoot aloft to trim the yards, according to the strength and direction of the wind. In changeable weather, constant attention was needed through the adjustment of the sheets with lines and halyards, men up high at work even when there was a howling snow storm, and the officers on watch almost needing an artist's eye to set the sails fair to wind.

The engine was held in reserve; it may have lacked flexibility and was slow to raise full steam even with the best quality coal. To boot, the mechanism, with steam power in its infancy, required a great deal of attention. But steam power proved vital to her survival in encounters with the ice and storms of Antarctic seas.

Writing by candlelight

Assistant steward Joe Matkin's letters home provide the only surviving account of the realities of a sailor's life 'below decks.' Joe, born in Rutland in 1853, was the son of a printer and stationer and well taught. His parents had put much store in their children's education. A life at sea was now considered a fair choice for a young man, with the days of press gangs long gone. By the 1850s the navy had much reformed its treatment of men to encourage recruitment. Joe joined the *Challenger's* victualling department as assistant steward, and kept a journal throughout the voyage, from which he composed his many letters home to his family.

His journal was written by candlelight while he stood at his desk in the poorly ventilated issuing room, down in the hold. It was the largest space he could call his own. He posted the journal home but it never reached its destination. However, his family preserved 69 of his letters, and in 1992 they were published in *At Sea with the Scientifics: The Challenger letters of Joseph Matkin.* His correspondence provides often meticulous descriptions of life on board seen through a sailor's eyes.

In the first letter to his cousin, Tom, Joe describes the early preparations for the voyage: 'Two light steam boats were shipped on board, and thirty miles of deep sea line and dredging line…All the scientists were busy stowing away their gear – thousands of small, air-tight bottles, little boxes packed in iron tanks for keeping specimens in. There's a photographic room on the main deck, and a dissecting room for carving up bears, whales, etc.' Joe often refers to the team of scientists as the 'Scientifics.'

It's from Joe's hand we learn of the plight of so many men in close quarters, of the accidents and fatalities, the desertions, the poor rations and the hardships. He exposes the gulf between the scientifics' work and the crew's long hours operating the 'drudge,' their disparaging term for the dredging and sounding equipment.

Soon after their return, a number of officers and scientists published their expedition diaries and log books. The first of these accounts was Assistant Chief Engineer William Spry's best-seller, *The Cruise of HMS Challenger, Voyages over many seas, scenes in many lands* (1876). Much of his writing covers operational matters, the care of the temperamental steam engines, the workings of the dredging and sounding apparatus. But, as *Challenger* stopped frequently for refuelling, provisions and refitting, he also describes the people they met, not just the welcome reception, the balls and dances the officers enjoyed among people of their own society, but the native peoples and their appearances. Of which more later.

Sub-Lieutenant Lord George Granville Campbell's *Log letters from the Challenger* (1881) provides a lyrical and often unsparing account of conditions at sea, with a candour not found in the formalities of the captain's log books. In early 1874, deep in the Southern Ocean, he tells of a snow storm driving the ship towards pack ice with 'the Captain and commander howling out orders from the bridge, hardly heard in the roaring wind, as the ship heads towards a berg, a towering, dim white mass looming grimly through the driving snow.' He comments that, 'Our trawlings and dredgings resulted in obtaining a vast number of invertebrate animals of every kind that live in the sea and of these, many thousands of species are new to science.' Yet he acknowledges that 'the bluejackets called the dredging operations by no other name than "drudging," which was not necessarily meant as satire, though it did convey their, and most of our, feelings!'

The naturalist Henry Nottidge Moseley set out to explore wherever the *Challenger* made landfall, on remote islands or stopovers to refuel or refit at the great seaports of Empire. He reckoned that the voyage had lasted 3 years and 155 days, and that 520 days were available for excursions ashore, including prolonged stays for a complete refit of the ship.

Moseley was most at home probing unlikely places for new specimens. And as the voyage progressed, he appears to have been increasingly drawn to the plight of native populations, especially the more remote island communities. This is reflected in the conclusions to his book, *Notes by a naturalist made during the voyage of HMS Challenger* (1879). 'On the surface of the earth, animals and plants and races of men are perishing rapidly day by day, and will soon be, like the Dodo, things of the past. The history of these things once gone can never be recovered. The loss will be most deeply felt in the field of anthropology, a science which is of higher importance to us than any other, as treating the development history of our own species. The languages of Polynesia are being rapidly destroyed or mutilated, and the opportunity of obtaining accurate information concerning these and the native habits of culture will have soon passed away.'

Sub-Lieutenant Herbert's account, *The voyage of the Challenger: a personal narrative of the historic circumnavigation of the globe in the years 1872-1876*, was published posthumously by his family in 1938. His private thoughts reveal the stresses of prolonged periods at sea, relieved, perhaps, by his drawings and watercolours. Swire, the last surviving *Challenger* officer, passed away in 1934, two years after Leading Stoker Charles Collings.

The Voyage of HMS *Challenger*

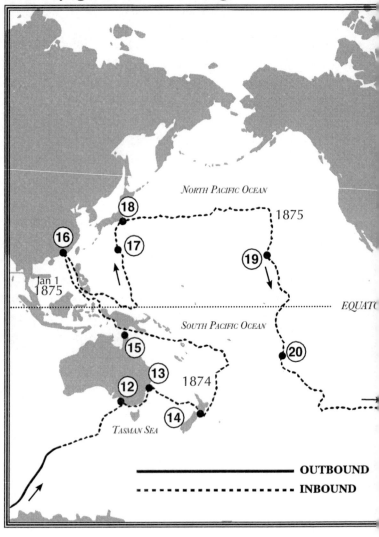

1. Portsmouth
2. Madeira
3. Halifax
4. San Miguel
5. St Vincent
6. St Paul's Rocks
7. Bahia
8. Inaccessible Island
9. Simonstown.
10. Kerguelen Island
11. Furthest Point South
12. Melbourne

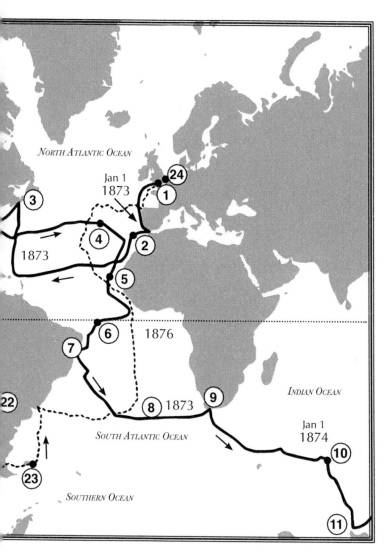

2

Into the Atlantic

On 21 December 1872, *Challenger* sailed from Portsmouth straight into a storm riding in from the Bay of Biscay. In one of his first letters, Joe writes, 'We went out through the Needles from Portsmouth & saluted the Queen at Osborne House as we passed. We had a head wind down Channel, & we have had a week of awful knocking about and half of us were sick for the first 2 or 3 days. The coal will only last til Lisbon, where we expect to arrive on 1 January, a week longer than we should have been…We had a miserable Xmas, for the ship was pitching and rolling and we had to hang on to our crockery and ware for grim death.'

'The crew were put on man-o-war rations, despite the ship's near full disarmament. The officers and Scientifics were set to have a grand dinner on Christmas Day. But first a turkey and then on Boxing Day a goose very mysteriously disappeared before they could reach the Captain's table…Some fragments of a goose and some salt were found this morning up in the main top rigging where the goose had been taken and devoured. The officers made a kick up about them, but can't find out who

'Farewell, HMS *Challenger*.' *Challenger* Report.

takes them... I should have liked to have helped pick a bit myself, for I have never been so hungry as the last few days, for we are now on a regular man-o-war diet & it's bringing some of us down a good deal.'

However, a brass band was soon assembled from volunteers drawn mainly from the seamen and marines. 'The officers bought the instruments & provided the Bandmaster to teach them' Joe writes. 'There were 15 volunteers & 9 wanted to play the big drum. They practise every day in the fore peak & the noise is something fearful and causes the watch below to swear a good deal.'

The *Challenger's* watches

At sea, the *Challenger's* crew followed an unbending daily routine based on seven watches over a 24-hour period, described in Navigating Sub-Lieutenant Herbert Swire's diary:

Morning watch	4 am to 8 am
Forenoon watch	8 am to 12 noon
Afternoon watch	12 noon to 4 pm
First dog watch	4 pm to 6 pm
Second dog watch	6 pm to 8 pm
First watch	8 pm to midnight
Middle watch	Midnight to 4 am

The officers were rostered to lead sets of four watches. For example, the officer of the afternoon watch was released when the watch sounds 4 pm, and is back on duty at midnight.

For the scientists, *Challenger* was a floating laboratory where, at their desks in their workrooms on the rolling sea, they would be analysing the results of dredging, sampling and sounding the world's oceans, or the returns from expeditions on shore. The Admiralty's Hydrographic Department issued a code of instructions defining the route and regulating the daily round of measurements to be made whenever the weather and circumstances permitted. Once the ship arrived at the spot to be sounded, the ship hove to and measurements of depth, temperature and salinity began. Soundings were taken at regular 200 mile intervals, at some 362 stations in total. The dredgings retrieved from the sea floor were recorded in the Station Book and forensically examined. More than 2,500 new marine species were identified.

Ship's dredging platform, *Challenger* Report.

Chemical laboratory on the *Challenger*.
***Challenger* Report.**

Wiki commons under CC license.

For some stretches of the voyage, such as between Australia and New Zealand, the course followed potential routes of submarine telegraph lines.

The New Year 1873 saw the first sea trials of the dredging apparatus begin off the coast of Lisbon. *Challenger* was now sailing in calmer waters, but the outward bound storm had left its legacy.

'We passed in the Bay of Biscay a vessel bottom upwards in the water, but it was too rough to lower a boat although we passed her quite close,' Joe writes. 'Again, we passed the remains of another vessel and a great quantity of oranges floating on the water, evidently one of the many fruit schooners running between here and England and had foundered in the gale with all hands on board.'

And as the first soundings began, so Joe begins to describe the work at hand. 'Cast the dredge again today to the bottom at 1800 fathoms, nothing came up in the dredge, showing the bottom to be rock. In hauling up a second time, the Lead and 300 fathoms more Line was lost over board. All day again we were dredging and obtaining the deepest bottom yet ascertained, at 2550 fathoms or nearly three miles, but in hauling up, the dredge and 1,700 fathoms of line was lost overboard, so that no criterion could be formed of the nature of the bottom.' The official report speculates that the dredge had caught on a telegraph cable.

But a workable and more reliable dredging routine was soon established. Steam power was an essential part of the operation. 'The first thing to be done,' writes engineer Spry, 'is to shorten and furl all sail and bring the ship head to wind, regulating her engine speed in such a manner as to avoid forcing her through water.' With the ship held steady in position at the sounding station, the screw turning slowly, work could then begin.

Sub-Lieutenant Swire led the sounding operations designed to measure the depth and other conditions of the oceans. The sailors assembled the inch-thick depth-sounding lines, stacking them on deck in reels 3000-fathoms long (about three and a half miles). Then, a self-closing loop designed to scrape up samples from the sea floor was tied to the end of the line.

Three men on deck of the H.M.S. *Challenger* studying Medusae, (jellyfish).

Next, a series of thermometers and sampling bottles were attached at intervals to measure the ocean's depth, temperature and salinity levels. The line, weighted down by heavy cast iron sinkers, was paid out by an 18 horse power winding engine fixed to the sounding platform above the main deck. The line was restrained by passing it through heavy iron blocks bolted to the deck. With red and blue coloured markers at 25 and 100 fathom intervals, the line was paid out until it came to rest on the sea bed, so revealing the ocean's depth. The weights were then released by the operation of a butterfly valve, as the strain of pulling the sinkers back up would cause the line to snap, as it sometimes did. The line was then hauled back up by men and machine, the instruments detached, the measurements and samples logged and pored over by the scientifics.

Thicker, weightier cables were required to dredge the ocean floor in deep water, coiled in lengths of up to 4,000 fathoms and spliced together. A cast iron dredging basket swept the deep sea bed for samples of small animal life, coral, sponges and rock. To ease the great strain on the cable itself, lengths of elastic India rubber were attached at intervals along the line, to help prevent the cable from reaching its breaking point.

A song for the *Challenger's* crew: February 1873

News of the early losses of dredging baskets and huge lengths of cable in the Mid-Atlantic soon reached the London newspapers via the submarine telegraph. In February 1873, Joe writes from Madeira, a parcel arrived in the mail from London addressed to 'the best Singer on board.' It contained a sea shanty, A Song for the *Challenger's* Crew. The writer was anonymous, but the lyrics survive because Joe copied out all nine verses. The song runs:

> *Old David Locker stole our dredge,*
> *To study well its form,*
> *Whilst we were fishing on the Ridge,*
> *Where all his Imps are born.*
>
> *So never mind your Dredge, my boys,*
> *Which you have lost below;*
> *Our country now your power employs,*
> *That man may wiser grow.*
>
> *Three cheers my boys, three jolly cheers,*
> *Our captain to inspire;*
> *His glorious staff knows no fears,*
> *Their souls are now on fire.*
>
> *So never mind your Dredge, my boys,*
> *Which you have lost below;*
> *Our country now your power employs,*
> *That man may wiser grow.*

The song urges the men to carry on dredging, for 'England now expects each man/His duty to perform/To carry out our Captain's plan/The future to adorn.'

The sea shanty singers, The Boarding Party, issued a recording of the song in 2003.

Boy Sailor Stokes: March 1873

But, as the voyage stretched out into the Atlantic, so the sounding depths increased and with it the strain on the blocks securing the cables to the ship. In March 1873, during dredging operations out in the mid-Atlantic, the stress on the dredging line was so severe that it tore away a restraining iron capstan bolted into the deck. Joe writes:

'The block, as it flew up, struck a Sailor Boy named Stokes on the head & dashed him to the deck with such a terrible force that his thigh was broken, and spine dreadfully injured. He was carried to the Sick Bay, and attended to by the Surgeons, but he was insensible the whole time and only lived two hours. At 5 pm the next day, the Bell tolled for his funeral, all the ship's company and the Officers and the scientific gents attending on the Main deck. The Captain read the service and at the appointed place in it, the body was lowered into the sea by the lad's messmates, three 36lb shots attached to it, to sink it, the depth was over four miles. The boy came from Deal where his Father is a Channel Pilot. All his clothes and effects were sold, and the money, with his wages, a few Photos, letters & his Bible, will be sent to his friends by this same mail.'

Engineer Spry recalls in his diary: 'After evening quarters, the bell tolled and all the ship's company assembled to pay their last tributes to their late shipmate. The Captain read the beautiful and appropriate service for the burial at sea, and on reaching the portion, 'We commit his body to the deep,' it was slid out of the port, wrapped in a hammock weighted with shot, into the bright blue tide, to be seen no more til that day when the sea shall give up its dead.'

The *Challenger's* muster book merely notes that Boy Sailor Stokes died of 'concussion of the brain.' His bible and few remaining possessions were remitted home, along with the proceeds of the sale. In his medical report of the voyage, the Surgeon records the incident: 'The dredging rope broke as he was stepping across it and it dashed him violently against the hammock settings.' He sustained a severe injury of the brain and lived only a few hours afterwards. In April 1873 a memorial stone was erected on the island of Bermuda in memory of 'Wm. H Stokes, 1st Class Boy,' together with a memorial for the late Adam Ebbels, the naval schoolmaster for the captain's young son, who had also recently passed away.

The following morning, dredging and sounding resumed, the task ahead to sound a 2,700-mile section of the North Atlantic from Tenerife to the Virgin Islands. According to Spry, *Challenger* hove to more than 20 times along this potential route for a transatlantic telegraph cable, to sample the ocean's depth, sea floor geology, ocean temperatures, and marine life. The stoppages were one to two hundred miles apart, occurring each day, weather permitting.

The dredge basket now began to bring treasures to the surface. Early in 1873, from samples retrieved off the Gibraltar coast, Professor Wyville Thomson identified a live specimen of a delicately spun sponge, the Venus Flower Basket (*Euplectella subarea*), a species found in the fossil record, previously only known in the deep waters of the Philippines. Spry describes it as 'an object most beautiful in form…the walls are of the most delicate tissue, recalling spun glass, resembling the finest transparent lace.' Together with finds of deepwater fish unknown to science, these findings confirmed that the sea floor was a haven for species previously thought to be extinct. Then, in a further discovery, the dredge began to retrieve from the sea floor potato-shaped nodules of a metallic rock. Testing the samples in his laboratory, Buchanan found them to be manganese-rich, but he was unable to explain their complex origin.

Euplectella subarea
Venus flower basket, *Challenger* Report.

Meanwhile, from the soundings taken during the long traverse of the North Atlantic sea bed, *Challenger* discovered the formation of the Mid-Atlantic Ridge, a submarine ridge lying along the north-south axis of the Atlantic Ocean. It rises from the sea floor at the central part of the Atlantic basin and runs equidistant between the continents on either side. The ridge is in effect an immensely long but mostly submerged mountain chain extending for about 10,000 miles in a curving path from the Arctic Ocean to near the southern tip of Africa. Its peaks sometimes reach above sea level, in the islands or island groups on or near the ridge, including the Azores, St Helena, St Paul's, Inaccessible Island and Tristan da Cuhna.

The ridge rises to between 2 to 3 km above the ocean floor, with a rift valley at its crest, marking the location at which the great tectonic plates of the Atlantic are slowly inching apart, apparently at about the rate it takes for fingernails to grow.

As *Challenger* cruised westward across the Atlantic and the soundings became ever deeper, the scientists also noted that the white ooze they were lifting from the sea bed was gradually changing in colour and texture from white to grey to deep red. The transition began at about 1,500 fathoms. Looking for an explanation for the change, fellow scientist John Young Buchanan experimented by pouring a weak acid solution onto a sample of the white ooze. He saw that within minutes the carbonate of lime in the sludge had dissolved, leaving a reddish mud. As Richard Corfield puts it, the explanation now known to science is that 'the acidity of the oceans increases with depth. Imagine, he writes, 'that the undersea mountains have the equivalent of a snow line, and you have an excellent image of what Wyville Thomson and the rest of his team had discovered.' But Wyville Thomson could only observe the change brought about by the experiment on board; deep in the ocean it was taking place 'by some means or other.'

'Common shipmates'

It's clear from his writings that Joe took a close interest in the results of the scientists' researches. But he also speaks of the widening gap between their quest for knowledge and the crew's labours to obtain it. Early on in the voyage, in an attempt to build bridges between scientists and crewmen, the captain asked Professor Thomson to address the men on the expedition's aims. Joe kept an account of his speech and quotes it in a letter home:

'It gives me great pleasure to do so,' he told the assembled crew, 'for we are to be common shipmates for the next few years, & doubtless each one has some interest in the work, &

the results, if successful, will be creditable to us all. In the first place, I must tell you that the bottom of the sea occupies an area three-quarters of the globe, & this immense portion has been as a sealed book to the human race.' Our ancestors did nothing to lift the veil, 'For it was thought that nothing living could exist at a greater depth than 400 fathoms,' a statement, he said, that had now been proved to be false.

He continued, 'It is now twenty years since scientific men began to talk of a scheme of Ocean telegraphs, whereby the continents of America and Europe might be placed in almost instantaneous communication. Some knowledge of the nature of the sea bottom was imperative to enable the cables to be laid with any degree of accuracy and safety.' Soundings were therefore taken at once across the Atlantic where the cable was to be laid, and other countries had carried on the research in a desultory manner. 'But it was at length decided by scientific men that no country but England, & none but British seamen, could solve the problem in anything like a satisfactory manner. The Chancellor of the Exchequer was consulted, & the result was that the *Challenger* & her crew were selected for the purpose.'

'We have obtained the deepest dredgings yet known to the world. Viz 3,175 fathoms, and from that depth have obtained specimens of animal life, proving that living creatures do exist in these great depths...the sea is teeming with animals of a sort hitherto unknown to man: animals nearly transparent but which have eyes, lungs and heart the same as we have.' He displayed various drawings by the artist, Mr Wild, of newly discovered creatures including a delicately drawn sea polyp 'half plant, half animal,' possessing the power to emit strong green light from its body. He then displayed a lobster, immense but without the bright eyes of a common lobster, 'for there is no light where the gentleman lives; no eyes he requires, for they would only be an encumbrance.'

Flattery may have helped improve morale, but communications remained poor. The British public would frequently learn of the *Challenger's* scientific accomplishments relayed through journals and popular newspapers well before the ship's crew.

Challenger completed its trans-Atlantic survey at Nova Scotia in April 1873 where she stopped to refuel and reprovision. She then turned southwards, heading for the Azores. She stopped at Bermuda in June 1873, but soon departed, for nearly the whole ship's crew suffered from dysentery. Two men were so ill they were left behind in hospital. 'Islands I never wish to see again,' Joe says. 'Two days after we had been to sea, all the mosquitoes and flies disappeared. Some of the sailors were covered in mosquito bites...my messmates who sleep on each side of me were almost driven mad by them every night, and could not understand why they didn't give me a turn.'

From Bermuda, *Challenger* passed through the Gulf Stream, putting in at the Azores island of San Miguel on 3 July 1873 for long-needed liberty, after weeks of sounding and dredging. 'It was like coming to an oasis in a desert,' Joe writes. 'The men have just returned on board, and it was worth sixpence to see them come up the ship's side and fall in for inspection. Very few could walk straight and several were rolling; being a Saturday night, a great many had brought off the materials for Sunday dinner, some had half a sheep on their backs, some pigs' heads, and large cheeses. A great many had lost their shoes & hats. All who could walk along the deck were set down as being drunk. Several lay down there and then and went to sleep, some excused themselves on the grounds that the ship was unsteady. These were all reported and had a day's leave stopped.'

The following afternoon, shore leave was again granted to all the men who could be spared. The wine shops were open as usual, the men called for pints, and soon got fighting in the main square. 'The soldiers had to be called out, and of course, this brought on a fight between the sailors and soldiers. The soldiers used their bayonets, and our men used stakes, wheelbarrows and anything they could get. The return to ship was worse than last night, & there has been any amount of fighting on deck since they came off; some are raving mad, and require 2 or 3 to hold them, but they will be alright tomorrow.'

And in July 1873, while all this is going on, hunched over his diary, Sub-Lieutenant Swire reflects: 'On board ship, they are only to be driven to do their work by inflicting summary punishment upon skulkers. They are constantly murmuring against those in authority, cannot be trusted in any capacity without an officer to superintend, and I verily believe, were it not for that ever excellent and never disgraced corps, the Royal Marine Light Infantry, would in the present state, be quite beyond the control of their officers...But enough, to tell the truth, my fingers ache. Having thus relieved my mind on this subject, let me make my peace with my brother sailors and endeavour to get on pleasantly with them.'

The seining party: August 1873

Challenger then resumed its trawling routines around the Cape Verde islands, retrieving many previously unknown creatures. They stopped for coal at St Vincent, and on 7 August 1873, took on provisions at St Jago, including two bullocks, 300 coconuts and 5,000 limes for the ship's company. Joe writes, 'One of the boys bought a monkey for nine shillings and sixpence, and let him run up the rigging. But he was made to chase it for three hours until he caught it, and then ordered to throw it overboard.'

Henry Moseley joined a shooting party in search of quail. They each selected a young lad from the town 'to carry our cartridge bags and show us where the quails and gallinis are to be found.' The entire party only shot about twenty quail, as few of these migratory visitors had yet to return to the island. So they directed their fire on the flocks of gallinis. But, he records that the birds 'station sentries to keep a look out from some rocky eminence, and once they have discovered an enemy, never lose sight of him, and give warnings as soon as he gets too near.'

That afternoon, Moseley's group returned to the town to join the *Challenger's* 'seining' party. 'All English men-o-war on foreign service are provided with a seine net,' he writes. The large fishing net is hung vertically in the water by weights at the lower edge and held up with floats on top. 'A seining party is regarded as a sort of lark or picnic by the Blue-jackets,' he adds. 'There are always plenty of volunteers eager to go, and a good many officers are ready to join.'

'With us, Mr Cox the boatswain was the great man on such occasions, and he enjoyed the sport as much as anyone in the ship. The party of volunteers, of perhaps thirty men besides the officers, goes ashore in the afternoon at about four o'clock in one of the cutters with the net in the dingy, the smallest ship's boat. Then the net is payed out, and everyone is dressed and prepared for going into the water up to his neck and hauling on the lines. At last, in comes the bag of the net, or "cod" as Mr Cox calls it. It is run up the beach with a final spurt, and then comes the fun of handing out the fish and looking at the many unfamiliar forms, for which the Blue-jackets have all sorts of extraordinary names.'

'At one haul there was a large shark *(Carcharis)* 14 feet long in the net. Mr Cox in the dingy, following the net as usual as it was drawn in, in order to free it if it should hitch on the bottom, sighted the shark swimming round within the ever decreasing circle, making bolts at the net to try and break through. And the beast would have burst through had not Mr Cox hammered it on the head with a boat hook, whilst the men belaboured it with anything they could get hold of as it got drawn into shallow water.'

'At last we ran the brute up high and dry. The sailor has absolutely no pity on the shark. I have heard one of our men say to a shark, which he had just hauled on to the forecastle with a line, "Ah, thou beggar, thou'd hurt I if I was in the water, and now I'll hurt thee."

'We caught plenty of fish. A fire had been lighted on the shore and we had a ship's boat's cooking stove with us. We fried some fish and with bread and preserved meats and plenty of beer made a good supper, and set to work again hauling the net until it had long been dark. Then we had hot tea and grog, and packed our net and fish into the boats and pulled on board.'

Ploughing through fire: August 1873

Challenger then went away to St Paul's Rocks, its next destination a group of five small, black volcanic peaks just north of the equator, white capped with sea birds' dung. 'For the last two nights,' Joe records, 'the sea has presented a wonderful phosphorescent appearance…the ship appears to be literally ploughing her way through fire, and the surface of the water is lighter than I have ever seen it on the brightest moonlit night.'

The rocks rise from an ocean floor far too deep for a conventional anchorage, so Captain Nares ordered long hawsers to be slung between the headlands of St Paul's. And with the ship rope anchored and held steady, Lieutenant Lord Campbell observes in his Log Letters From The *Challenger*:

'On the night of the 14th, the sea was most gloriously phosphorescent, to a degree unequalled in our experience. A fresh breeze was blowing and every wave and wavelet as far as one could see from the ship on all sides to the distant horizon flashed brightly as they broke...Astern of the ship, deep down where the keel cut the water, glowed a broad band of emerald green light, from which came streaming up myriads of yellow sparks, which glittered and sparkled against the brilliant cloud light below...it was as if the "milky way", as seen through a telescope, had dropped down on the ocean and we were sailing through it. That night it was light enough to read by.'

The light emanated from a newly identified, minute diatom, *Pyrocistis*, described in one the first scientific papers published by a *Challenger* scientist, John Murray, in the *Proceedings of the Royal Society of London*, 1876. Soundings around St Paul's Rocks also revealed unusually cold deep-water temperatures, which, as Campbell also wrote, 'all goes to prove the theory of the bottom water coming from the Antarctic and spreading right way up north.'

HMS *Challenger* at St. Paul's Rocks, *Challenger* Report.

Casting off from St Paul's, *Challenger* now stretched southwards to the equator, crossing the line at 1 pm on 30 August, 1873. Joe writes, 'The Captain issued wine to all hands in honour of the event.' But for those crossing the equator for the first time, 'no shaving etc was allowed,' Joe says, for the captain would not hold with the old ritual whereby first timers would have their heads and beards lathered with tar or rancid grease and shaved bald with a piece of barrel hoop before being ducked.

In September 1873, with only a few buckets of coal remaining in the hold, *Challenger* docked at the Brazilian port of Bahia Bay. On the quay, Joe witnessed the brutal ill treatment of enslaved men whom the captain hired to load the coal. Brazil continued to import Africans, legally and illegally, well into the nineteenth century before officially ending slavery in 1888. Bahia alone imported more than 1,300,000 men, women, and children. More than 90 percent of the Africans who arrived in Bahia came from either the Bight of Benin or central Africa.

Usually, *Challenger's* steam-powered winch would hoist fuel sacks aboard. But in Bahia, cheap labour was readily available. Joe writes, 'The greater part of these negroes are slaves, and are let out for hire by their masters for about 6d per day. We had about 60 of them getting in our coal while the ship's company went on leave, and they got in 200 tons in one day. They live chiefly on Manioc flour, the same root from which tapioca is made.' Later, observing the Brazilian navy ships anchored nearby, he says, 'The seamen are nearly all negroes, and are thrashed a good deal at times.'

Returning to his diary after a day going about the city, Sub-Lieutenant Swire presumed to write: 'Of course, In England, slavery is looked upon with great abhorrence, but were the facts of the case properly known I think this feeling would be much modified: the negroes are by nature a lazy race and will not work unless made to; they are undoubtedly an inferior race; they as a rule do not wish to become free, being well treated; and in nearly every country where the slaves have been unconditionally liberated the crops and the country produce have gone to rack and ruin… There are some regulations concerning slave children which I did not quite catch; if slavery by inheritance be not abolished, it will take the slaves long to free themselves by purchase or by other means.'

Moseley had taken the trouble to be a little better informed: 'A law is now in force by which every child born in the country is free, and further, a master is obliged to free a slave if the slave can raise a sufficient sum to buy himself off. The amount to be paid is fixed by the government valuer, and the sum fixed is low as Slaves commonly buy themselves off. A Society exists which assists them to do so, advancing the money on loan and receiving it back by instalments…As a result, the value of slaves has fallen very much.'

'But slaves are hired out as servants, and foreign residents, especially the English, who cannot hold slaves, hire them as domestic servants. They pay them their wages, and the slaves carry these wages to their owners, who, if kind, give them a fourth part or so as a present.' A German hotel proprietor told Moseley that hiring was 'much better than buying slaves, since when they were ill, you sent them back to their owners and got fresh ones.'

3

Southern Ocean sailing

On 25 September 1873, *Challenger* left Bahia for Cape Town by way of Tristan Da Cuhna, its hold full of coal and extra sacks on deck for the long voyage ahead. Sounding and sampling began of a new section of the ocean as she beat south and eastwards towards Da Cuhna. Occasionally, they would come across a barnacle-covered fragment of timber and haul it aboard for inspection for any living creatures it carried. 'Only two vessels have been passed since leaving Bahia,' Joe writes to his cousin, Tom, 'for this part of the ocean is not often crossed, the only living companion we have are Albatrosses, Cape hens, Cape Pigeons and Petrels and a host of other sea birds. The Albatross is the monarch of birds, frequently measuring 17 feet from wing to wing, and in flying does not flap his wings but keeps them spread out. These birds will follow a ship for miles in cold latitudes & have very powerful wings and beaks.'

Albatrosses like to follow ships, maybe because evolution has encouraged them to follow whales across the ocean, scavenging the remains of squid or fish that fall from the mouth of these messy eaters. And when the wind is not with them, they can use it all the same to pursue their course, to lift them high above the sea and then allow gravity to glide them rhythmically downwards in the direction they need to go.

Their constant presence would seem like a bad omen for crewmen faced with constant danger in hostile waters. Joe's next entry takes up this theme: 'Some years ago, HMS *Sutledge* on her way to Vancouver's island lost a man overboard in a gale of wind; a boat was lowered but just before it reached him, an Albatross swooped down & drove its beak into his skull, killing him on the spot.'

Then he quotes the fateful lines from Coleridge's *Rhyme of the Ancient Mariner*, describing the calamities which followed a ship among ice and snow when a seaman shot the bird down with his bow: 'With his cruel blow he laid him low/The harmless albatross.'

Bob Watson's shanty, Mollymawk, captures the great bird's haunting presence:

> *Well, the Southern Ocean is a lonely place,*
> *Where the storms are many and the shelter scarce,*
> *Down upon the Southern Ocean sailing,*
> *Down below Cape Horn.*
>
> *On the restless water and the troublin' skies,*
> *You can see that mollymauk wheel and fly.*
> *Down upon the Southern Ocean sailing,*
> *Down below Cape Horn.*
>
> *Won't you ride the wind and go, white seabird,*
> *Ride the wind and go, mollymauk.*
> *Down upon the Southern Ocean sailing,*
> *Down below Cape Horn.*
>
> *He's the ghost of a sailor-man as I've heard say,*
> *Whose body sank, and his soul flew away.*
> *And he's got no haven and he's got no home,*
> *He's bound evermore for to wheel and roam.*

When I gets too weary for to sail no more,
Let my bones sink better far away from shore.
You can cast me loose and leave me driftin' free,
And I'll keep that big bird company.

A month later, in mid-October 1873, Tristan Da Cuhna hove in sight, its peak a mass of snow and ice rising to 8,300 feet. In the shelter of the island, *Challenger* dropped anchor offshore to take on fresh water and provisions. Beneath the mountain, little habitable land was available save for an extensive grassy slope above the anchorage, on which were built the inhabitants' white walled cottages. Joe reckoned that the islanders numbered some 86 men, women and children. 'Sheep, cattle, pigs, geese and fowls they have in plenty, also potatoes and other vegetables, all of which they sell to passing traders who give them flour or money in exchange. The whole male population came off in their boats,' Joe writes, 'bringing with them potatoes, albatross eggs &c. They were dressed in various costumes and wore sealskin shoes.'

Rescue: October 1873

While ashore for their purchases and entertainment, the crew gathered from the islanders' hearsay that two German mariners, Gustave and Frederiche Stoltenhoff, were marooned some way offshore, on Inaccessible Island. It was said that two years ago or more, a whaling ship had landed the brothers on the island to make their fortune hunting for seal furs and oil, while their ship went south in search of whales in Antarctic waters. The ship was due to return to pick them up a few months later, but had failed to do so. The whaler was thought to have foundered in the ice. The Da Cuhnans became acquainted with the brothers out there on the rock while seal hunting for themselves. But it became evident to the *Challenger's* men, judging from the islanders' indifference bordering on hostility, that the brothers had been abandoned to their fate. Some Da Cuhnans appeared to believe the brothers had set up a rival trading post for passing ships.

Inaccessible Island lay some 20 miles away on the western horizon. Perhaps in response to the crew's concerns for the men's plight, for the island was not on his itinerary, Captain Nares ordered *Challenger* to get underway. At night as the ship steamed slowly towards the island, the ship's log records: 'Observed a light on Port bow. Burnt a blue light. Mist.' Early next morning she anchored off the northern side of Inaccessible Island.

Campbell describes 'a magnificent wall of black cliff splashed green with moss and ferns, rising sheer 1,300 feet above the sea…with hundreds of mollymawks and gulls soaring above, or resting on its face, and beneath it a strip of stony beach. At the foot of the beach we saw a hut, and soon afterwards, the Germans.'

As the ship hove to, Moseley writes, 'All night the penguins were to be heard screaming on shore and about the ship, and as parties of them passed by, they left vivid phosphorescent tracks behind them as they dived through the water alongside…as we approached the shore, I was astonished at seeing a shoal of what looked like extremely active very small porpoises or dolphins…. they showed black above and white beneath, and came along in a shoal of about fifty or more from seawards towards the shore at rapid pace, by a series of successive leaps out of the water and splashes into it again, describing short curves in the air, taking headers out of the water and headers into it again, til they went splash through the surf on to the black stony beach and there struggled and jumped up amongst the boulders and revealed themselves as wet and dripping penguins, for such they were.'

Stoker Collings was one of the dozen sailors and officers sent to the brothers' rescue. A group photograph (see page 146) captures the crew and the two German brothers in front of the mariners' grass hut.

Gustav Stoltenhoff, the younger of the two brothers, had already spent time on Tristan Da Cuhna, where he had landed with the surviving crew of his ship, the *Beacon Light*, which had been lost by fire some 300 miles to the west of the island. On returning home, Gustav persuaded his older brother that there was a living to be made there from seal hunting and barter with passing ships. They booked as passengers on board of a whaler, the *Java*, bound for South Atlantic waters. But the captain's account of the settlers dissuaded them from landing on Da Cuhna. He described Inaccessible Island as a fertile place, the seats of seal and sea elephant fisheries, with an abundance of wild goats and pigs.

The brothers landed on Inaccessible Island in November 1871. Before he set off, the whaler's captain had provided them with a store of sugar, coffee, flour, vinegar, tobacco, a whale boat, a rifle and ammunition, cooking utensils, vegetable seeds, two blankets each, and spars and glazed windows for a shelter. The brothers built their hut at the back of a narrow strand at the foot of a perpendicular granite cliff, near a waterfall. While still waiting for their ship to return, they would scale the cliff or row round the far side of the island to hunt for wild goats and boar. However, their boat was damaged in a storm the following winter, and their remaining provisions were so much reduced that by mid-summer both men were but little more than skeletons.

Their whaler never returned and was in all probability lost. A few vessels passed by, some agreeing to small exchanges of seal skins and blubber for flour and other provisions, others failing to respond to the brothers' smoke signals. Meanwhile, on their hunting trips to the island, the Da Cuhnans turned hostile once they realised that the Stoltenhoffs were encroaching on their trade. In Swire's account of the brothers' plight, he writes:

'Shortly after they landed they were visited by men from Tristan d'Acuhna who, they say, shot their seven goats which they had near their house, drank nearly all their store of tea, stole their tools and made themselves as objectionable as possible in order to drive them from an island where they were thought likely to disturb the seals which the Tristan people have learned to look on as their own. After this visit they were reduced to great straits, and nearly starved. They had no boat and to get from one part of the shore to the other they had to swim.' The brothers devised a plan whereby one would climb to the top of the precipitous cliff and whenever he was able to shoot a wild pig or goat he cut it in half, pitched it down to his brother and kept the half for himself. 'At last no more were left and they had to confine themselves to stray pigs, birds and eggs. They only just managed to keep body and soul together, their boots were worn out and they had to go barefoot over the sharp rocks and freezing seas.'

'When we hove in sight they were immensely delighted, as may be imagined, for they had made many signals to passing vessels but none had noticed them, so that when they saw a steamer coming in straight for their hut their feelings must have been of delirious joy.'

Swire was one of the rescue party, along with Stoker Collings and ten others. They found the brothers starving and in rags, without flour, rice, potatoes or vegetables, surviving on penguins' eggs.

Joe writes that, before leaving the island the Stoltenhoffs set fire to their hut, 'so that the Tristan people, to whom they bear no good will, may not benefit from it in any of their seal hunting excursions.' After hearing of their story, the Captain consented to give them passage to the Cape, 'and has given them some clothes & c. for their own were quite worn out, and they had neither boots nor stockings.' In William Spry's account, 'after a good breakfast, they were able to tell their own story,' which he reproduces in his book.

As *Challenger* headed for the Cape, Joe writes: 'The Germans are getting fat. One of them is reading *Sketches by 'Boz'*, the other *Nicholas Nickleby*.'

Deserters: October 1873

On 28 October 1873, after 10 months of surveying the Atlantic Ocean, *Challenger* dropped anchor in Simon's Bay, some 24 miles by road from Cape Town. The stresses of the dredging operations were already showing in the numbers of crewmen deserting the ship. 'The men are very dissatisfied at not getting extra pay for this cold weather trip,' Joe says, 'and the work is so much harder for everyone than in an ordinary man-o-war, when the ship is in harbour six months at a time…. but now when we go into harbour it's to refit, coal or provision and the men get scarcely any leave. Several of the officers are great bullies, the most popular of the lot is Lord Campbell.'

'Several of our men wish to leave the ship here…the work is too hard and the sea time so long…men also to be invalided home as they cannot stand the many sudden changes of climate experienced on this ship.' The vessel's close confinement (a mere 200 feet long and 40 feet wide) added to the stress, and the 'endless grind of dredging the seabed and retrieving what looked to the untutored eye lumps of mud.'

Challenger bluejackets rescue the marooned Stoltenhoff brothers.

…rlie Collings is back row, third from the left. One brother is to his left, the other …s a pipe. *Challenger* collection, National Maritime Museum, Greenwich.

By the time the ship was ready to depart, Joe records that 'two more men have deserted and three are now absent. One boy tried to swim ashore last night, & has never been heard of since, the distance was 1 ¼ mile, & it was blowing hard, & the boy had his clothes on.'

Half of the ship's company were sent off with four days' leave, while the remaining crew were dismantling the ship for refitting, and soon every yard and spar was on deck except the topmasts and crossyard jack.

Moseley set out on a fortnight's walking holiday upcountry in Wynberg. 'The officers liked Cape Town for its gaiety and dancing. I enjoyed Simons Bay most thoroughly, because it is a place where one can get at once amongst wild nature and over the hills and moors.' Here, he made one of the most important zoological discoveries of the voyage. Ever inquisitive, he discovered beneath an old cart-wheel in the garden of his hotel a live specimen of a black caterpillar, *Peripatus*. Three inches long, the creature is a 'missing link' between two species, having the body of an earthworm, but the appendages of an insect, with seventeen pairs of short, conical feet, each with a pair of hooked claws. Moseley dissected the specimen in his laboratory, finding that the animal breathes air by means of tracheal tubes, like those of insects. 'I found only vegetable matter in the stomachs of the *Cape Peripatus*, and concluded that it was a vegetable eater…They have a remarkable power of extension of the body, and when walking, stretch to nearly twice the length they have when at rest.' Its antecedents were later found in the earliest fossil records.

Meanwhile, on December 8th, in appreciation of their warm reception into Cape society, the officers held a ball at the Exchange Hall in Cape Town, inviting more than 400 guests. The ship's band was playing and the ballroom decorated with flags and *Challenger's* dredge apparatus on display, with two

CAPE TOWN
DECEMBER 8TH 1873.

National History Museum, *Challenger* archives.

sailors in their whites on guard alongside. They were so drunk by midday they had to be relieved by two others. Joe mailed a copy of the ball's programme to his mother. The sketch on the programme's cover (see above) represents the dredge on the sea bed and two mermaids examining it and taking out a starfish. 'It will give you an idea of what the dredge looks like,' he tells his mother. 'The appendages on the bottom of the dredge are for catching up aneroids, insects &c.'

One day, on shore leave, Joe walks alone to the top of Table Mountain, describing the view south to the Dutch town of Wynberg and the vineyard country around it, and beyond that, the mountains around Simon's Bay 'until you came around and saw the city of Cape Town spread out under your feet.'

He describes two merchant ships and their human cargo anchored far off the Cape shore, 'been and gone since we were here, they were called Emigrant Ships, & each had on board about 500 coolies from Calcutta for Jamaica and Demerara, to work in the sugar plantations there. They go for five years and are paid 2d a day, are supposed to be voluntarily emigrating, but it really is a quiet way of importing slaves, for they are treated like those in the West Indies and very few ever live to get back to India again. The ships lie a long way from shore and don't allow their emigrants to land, neither permit anyone on board. I was looking at them the other day through a telescope, they were dirty, miserable looking creatures all wrapped up in blankets having had cold weather beating round the Cape of Good Hope. They only remained four days to take in water, fresh provisions &c.'

Joe was writing more than sixty years after Parliament passed the Abolition of the Slave Trade Act, 1807, as a result of which the Royal Navy had played some part in suppressing the West African trade.

He went into town to buy boots and warm clothing for the long voyage south. 'My increase in pay will commence on 1 December, making £26 6s and 4d per annum. I have not been able to save anything yet, owing to the small pay & the lot of clothes I have had to buy, for we want Tropical clothes one month, & Arctic clothing the next.' And, in a rare personal aside, says, 'I invariably go on shore by myself. I have not a single companion in the ship – that I call a companion, though of course we are all sociable and friendly.'

His letter ends with a word about Wyville Thomson: 'He engaged a young Caffre for a servant in the Analysing room… he also has a Bermuda Negro for his private servant.' Southern Africa's white colonists used the word 'Caffre' to characterise the region's black majority as an inferior race of African origins. The ship's Photographer had also jumped ship. 'The police are after him,' Joe writes.

When he returned from shore leave, Sub-Lieutenant Swire found the refitting of the ship was progressing energetically.

'The topsail yards were already across and the topgallant masts pointed, and all the new running gear had been rove [secured]. Great preparations are now being made for the stretch south which we are to make after leaving here. Several extra stoves for warming the ship having been sent on board, and large supplies of clothing calculated to keep out the cold and wet having been forwarded to us from England. I have invested in a pair of sea boots, a sou'wester, a huge pair of mittens, and a thick monkey jacket, so I think I am pretty well provided with gear for battling with the element.'

'A crow's nest for the masthead man has been made of an old tub, so that the look-out man whom it is necessary to keep up there will not be unnecessarily exposed to cold.'

Salt pork and pea soup: December 1873

Now refitted, at first light on 17 December 1873, *Challenger* left the security of the Cape harbour and put out under steam for the Southern Ocean. The air grew colder and the barometer fell as the ship headed for a chain of inhospitable islands – Edward and Marion, the Crozets, Kerguelen and Heard. The first of these lies over 1,000 miles south of Cape Town. 'Our second Christmas on board has arrived and finds us in sight of two snow-covered islands,' Joe writes. 'All hands were on deck looking out for land until dinner time, when the Band struck up *The Roast Beef of Old England*, which sounded very nice, though dinner was salt pork and pea soup. We brought our own private stores with us, and had a fine dinner, considering. The Captain walks round, just to see the tables laid out, and tastes each mess's plum duff, a very ancient custom in the Navy. There are twenty messes but he only managed about five. After, about one third of a pint of Madeira was issued to each man, and the band played dance music, which they are still doing, so I being no dancer have got this letter under weigh.'

'We too had a grand dinner,' Swire writes'. All the officers of the ship mustering in the ward room at six o'clock, when the feast commenced. The band played at intervals during the evening, and after dinner we all mustered on the main deck to smoke, when someone having started a song, all the rest joined in and once started the singing continued until a late hour, much whisky being consumed meanwhile.'

Yet, as the new year rolled in, the dredge and sounding lines were back in operation. The *Challenger* Report records that, on 29 and 30 January 1873, 'between one and two hundred animals belonging to nearly all the marine groups were taken in each of the hauls, and with few exceptions, they belonged to genera and species discovered for the first time by the Expedition.' Deposits retrieved at 1,375 fathoms comprised seven new genera and 25 new species. A whiteish *Globigerina* ooze was retrieved from the ocean floor, containing 81% of carbonate of lime, the residue being almost wholly the remains of diatoms and radiolarians, different forms of algae and minute globe-shaped sea shells accumulating on the seabed.

The officers, sailors and at least some of the scientists had very quickly became bored with the dredge retrieving seemingly endless quantities of white mud from the sea floor. Yet understanding the nature and origin of ocean floor sediments was one of the expedition's crucial scientific goals. Before setting out on the cruise, Professor Thomson had firmly believed that the plankton forming the white *Globigerina* ooze retrieved from the dredge had lived and died on the sea floor iself, where it would form into chalk. But his fellow scientist, John Murray, contended that the plankton lived at or near the surface of the sea. The seabed deposits were formed by the 'rain' of dead plankton as the shell-secreting creatures died and their shells drifted down to the sea floor. As the survey evidence accumulated, so Thomson conceded, admitting to his error in an academic paper for the Royal Society drafted at sea as they voyaged south towards the 'Great ice Barrier', now known as the Ross Ice Shelf.

Challenger made perhaps the first systematic analysis of the sediments on the ocean floor. For the modern day oceanographer, there is little to match the information on the earth's recent history to be found trapped in these accumulating deposits, their composition of algae and minute shells mirroring fluctuations in the earth's climate and the changing condition of the oceans, described by Richard Corfield as a 'library of time.'

Christmas Harbour: January 1874

On 7 January 1874, *Challenger* next found a safe anchorage in Christmas Harbour on Kerguelen's Land. The explorer Captain James Cook had named it Desolation Island during his visit a hundred years before, with its high black fringing cliffs and snowfields on bleak volcanic mountains. But the island offered *Challenger* the sheltered bay Cook had chosen, perhaps the best in the whole Southern Ocean. Kerguelen cabbage grew in abundance on the island, the favourite food of the Kerguelen teal, a small brown duck with a metallic blue streak. Many were killed by the seamen as they went ashore, for as Mosley writes, 'Only those who have been long at sea know what an intense craving for fresh meat is developed.' Rising away from the beach, the peaty earth beneath the dense verdant carpets of azorella was perforated everywhere with holes of ground-nesting prions and petrels. 'On several occasions,' he writes, 'I superintended parties of stokers, who volunteered to dig up birds and eggs for our collection.'

At anchor, Christmas Harbour, January 1874: HMS *Challenger*, Report.

Mosley then observes, 'An idea of the relations between various birds in the struggle for existence will be gained from the following: I saw a cormorant rise to the surface of the water and lifting its head, made desperate efforts to gorge a small fish, evidently knowing its danger, and in a fearful hurry to get it down. Before it could swallow its prey, down came a gull, snatched the fish after a slight struggle, and carried it off to the rocks on the shore. And here, as lots of other gulls began to assert their right to a share, when down swooped a skua from aloft, right on the heap of gulls, and seized the fish and swallowed it at once.'

'The shag ought to learn to swallow under water, and the gull to devour its prey at once in the air.'

The expedition fell in with two whaling ships, the *Rosswell King* and the *Emma Jane*, already at anchor in Christmas Harbour. Captain Nares invited their skippers to dine with his officers almost every night, for he wanted to extract from them all the information he could regarding the island's topography and the navigation of the surrounding seas. And in line with the Admiralty's instructions, Captain Nares spent three weeks surveying the island, some 70 miles long and 10 miles wide. 'The walking was frightful,' Joe writes, 'the island is one vast swamp, at every other step you sink up to your knees in boggy ground.' The weather would change dramatically. While dredging and sounding off Christmas Harbour, 'We were struck by a very heavy sea which smashed the sounding platform & went down the funnel and into the stoke hole, frightening the engineers and stokers a good deal. They thought we had run into an ice berg.'

Here, too, they met a whaler from nearby Heard Island. 'The crew composed English, Scotch, Americans, Negroes, most of whom came on board before we left. They join the vessel for four years and are paid according to their success, but the average is much less than that of our men, while the hardship is something awful. They would gladly have changed places with ours; from the time they leave America until they return they scarcely see a strange face. These men have been here three years & the only inhabited place they have landed on is Tristan d'Acunha.'

'Once a year another vessel comes out to them bringing provisions, clothing, and taking back their oil and skins…When they kill a whale they take the blubber to the nearest island and boil it down. Casks are filled with oil and left there until the store vessel comes. They live very well, for they eat wild duck, albatross, penguins, sea elephants, sea leopards and any amount of cabbage.' Describing the whalers' slaughtering of sea elephants for their flesh and oil, Joe writes, 'The whalers generally spear them, and they tell us that, like the elephant on land, they often shed tears while dying, and look at you with such a pitiful and accusing gaze.'

Some days later, *Challenger* met up with two more American whalers, the *Imogen* and the *Royal King*. 'The two captains came on board our ship to dinner,' Joe says. 'Several of the crewmen of the vessels also came, & we had the band under weigh & some good dancing.'

Ice blink: February 1874

On 16 February, *Challenger* left Heard Island, heading further south, with a good breeze which increased to a regular gale during the night, so that, Joe writes, 'The ship was knocked about any how by the tremendous seas. Two of the main deck ports were stove in & men knocked out of their hammocks by the sea…there was 12 inches of snow on deck when we got up.' *Challenger* had now penetrated the outer reaches of the Antarctic Ice Barrier, where the ocean was fringed with sea ice and degrading icebergs. Joe writes, 'we had some job to get her out again. Her course was much impeded by great lumps of floating ice, & the roar they made against the bows during the night I shall never forget. It was like thunder more than anything else, & the grinding noise woke all who were in their hammocks, and nearly everyone was on deck.'

Yet, Joe says, 'It was a beautiful sight to see the ship ploughing her way thro' & the light emitted from the ice made it nearly as light as day. The light is called by Polar voyagers the Ice Blink. The Artist made sketches of most of the large ice bergs. We passed one on the night of the 14th which looked something like Windsor Castle, & had a large cavern through which it showed the daylight on the other side. Several looked like the Spithead Fort. Many had great fissures through them, as if stricken with Lightning, their rents were of a dark blue colour.'

Swire describes the ice blink as 'a peculiar light yellow in appearance which the sky assumes near the horizon when ice is in that direction, and from it may be judged pretty accurately the position and extent of the pack ice; if there are breaks in the blink it may be assumed that there are also breaks in the ice, and according to the colour and extent of these breaks, the practicability of the breaks in the ice may also be guessed. Ross, in his Antarctic cruise, soon found out the convenience of this ice blink, which told him many a time in which direction it was advisable to steer.'

Ship in ice, Kerguelen Island, *Challenger* Report.

'At the present moment, on deck, there is a grand example. The sun has sunk in the west about an hour ago, leaving behind a dense mass of dark clouds, overhanging an inky sea. Between the two, however, and extending up to about 2 degrees from the sea horizon, is a long streak of brilliant yellowish red light,

The band on HMS *Challenger*, Report: 'The noise is something fearful...'

throwing up in bold relief a rugged sea evidently of ice, for no waves that roam the sea were ever so fixed and rigid as these hummocks. Here and there a big berg can be distinguished, but between the broken ridges extends inexorably, so I fear we shan't get far in that direction tonight.'

And on that same day, 16 February, at latitude 66 degrees 39 minutes south, the captain 'issued wine to all hands to celebrate our entry into the Antarctic Circle. The barrier is still in sight,' Joe writes, 'and we are surrounded by icebergs of all sizes and shapes. There are also any amount of great Whales blowing and having such a game among themselves. It is now 10 pm and the sun is still above the horizon, & the sky lit like fire, giving all the icebergs to the West a scarlet tinge...We all wear our polar clothing, large caps with flaps to them to cover the ears and neck, and great jackets, trousers, boots & mitts. I am considered to look like the Shah of Persia in my cap. A great by-word among the men at present is, "Do you think you shall weather it Bill?" "Yes, I think I shall go round in her Bob."'

Meanwhile, in the confines of his cabin, Sub-Lieutenant Swire was describing the 'sheer monotony' of working through the ice. 'For my part, I am thoroughly sick of it, and ready to go north at a moment's notice. It is now more than two months since we left the Cape, and not having touched any inhabited land since then, we are beginning to ponder on the delights which await us in Australia.'

'We continue to enjoy the good things of life on board, though, not having yet been reduced to salt provisions. The men, of course, have to live on salt grub, but we have sheep still left, besides preserved meat and vegetables and wine, etc, in unlimited quantity. Another great advantage is being able to get as much water as we wish for, the usual allowance of one gallon each per diem not having been resorted to, so that we can still have our baths, etc as usual. Most of the fellows qualify their tubs with warm water, but I and a few other fellows stick religiously to cold, even with the thermometer ten degrees below freezing point.'

On 23 February, for Joe, the ocean came alive, with the 'magnificent sunset, and 45 icebergs were sighted all round, besides any amount of Penguins and Whales jumping about all around us. We sounded at 1,300 fathoms, and hove the dredge, when some good specimens were obtained.'

But, here in the far Southern Ocean, the winds blow freely westwards under the influence of the Earth's rotation. With no impeding landmasses, they can build suddenly and unexpectedly into some of the most fearsome waves in the world. Lieutenant Campbell writes that, 'The wind suddenly came on to blow fresh from the southward. The dredge was hive up in a hurry, by which time it was blowing a gale with heavy snow squalls and very thick weather.' All hands were called to make sail. 'The ship was steamed close under the lee of a large iceberg to allow the topsails to be reefed, and some under-current drifted her right on to the berg. The engines were turned full speed astern but to no purpose, & she drifted right onto it...with sufficient force to carry away the jib boom, dolphin striker and other head gear.'

'The men aloft, thinking they would have the top gallant mast about their ears, scurried down with extraordinary alacrity.'

Later that day, in dense fog, while the carpenters were repairing the damage, Joe describes a large iceberg 'discovered drifting right on to us. The hands were called to make sail, but by the time they got on deck, the berg was only 20 yards from us, and rose right above the ship's mast. The confusion was something fearful, nearly everyone was on deck, it was snowing and blowing hard all the time. One officer was yelling out one order, another something else. The engines were steaming full speed astern, and by hoisting the topsail, the ship shot past in safety. A seaman fell from the trysail while they were hoisting it and was much hurt...The captain and commander were howling out the orders from the bridge, hardly heard in the roaring of the wind; officers repeating the howls.'

The storm raged all night, and three lookouts were posted, with Captain Nares on deck the whole night, repeatedly ordering the ship to go about to avoid collisions or seek shelter in the lee of a berg. He had pushed his ship to the limits, averting disaster solely through the use of its steam power, and now the captain ordered her to turn away from the Antarctic, heading for Australia.

Australian welcome: March 1874

A month later, on 17 March 1874, *Challenger* anchored off Sandridge, the seaport suburb of Melbourne. Since leaving the Cape, they had been three months at sea, except for a few breaks ashore on the Kerguelen Islands. 'There was joy among us arriving at Melbourne,' Campbell writes. 'Of gales, snow, icebergs and discomfort generally, we had had enough, and the memory of the dinner I ate at the club the first evening, followed by the opera, yet lingers in my memory as one of the pleasantest of a poorly paid and laborious career! We lived at this club for more than a week. The members are a hospitable set of men, the mere fact that we were RN's being sufficient to ensure us invitations up country.'

During the ship's three-month stopovers in Melbourne and Sydney, Joe was reunited with friends from a previous voyage. 'Our men say Melbourne is the finest place in the world, they were so well treated by the people; the railway authorities gave them free passes for travelling up the country. Many went to Ballarat, the great gold mining metropolis, and 6 of them never came back. On 30 April, 2 seamen tried to escape from the ship to the shore in one of the boats, but they were re-captured and are now in irons waiting for the court martial.' The following day, Joe accompanied the Paymaster to draw £800 from the bank to pay the ship's company.

And, here, exploring the Australian outback, Moseley began to reveal his growing interest in anthropology. On an excursion from Melbourne, Mosley remarks on 'one of the most curious sights in the bush, that of the ancient tracks of the Aborigines up the trees, climbed by them to obtain possums or wild honey. These tracks are a series of small notches made by three blows of the tomahawk to admit the great toes and thus act as a ladder to the Black man. The tracks, which are to be seen everywhere in Australia, lead to the most astonishing heights.'

Yet the naturalist's objectivity then deserts him. Echoing Huxley's dictum, that no rational man would believe the average negro 'will be able to compete successfully with his bigger-brained and smaller-jawed rival,' Moseley comments: 'Marvellous as this power of climbing with so little support is, it can be done by Whites, and I was assured in New South Wales that there was a White man in the neighbourhood who could beat any Black at this sort of climbing, doing it in exactly the same way, and being often employed by my informant in collecting wild honey for him at so much a nest. In the same way, there are said to be Whites who can throw the boomerang better than any Blacks. In fact, a White man, when he brings his superior faculties to bear on the matter, can always beat a savage in his own field, perhaps even tracking.'

He visits a government reserve where 'a number of aborigines are maintained at Government expense under a missionary. There are about 120 Blacks there. They live in a small village of rough wooden houses or bark houses, in the midst of which is the house of Mr Green, the superintendent.'

'The Blacks have been lately employed in cultivating hops, and with tolerably good success, but are incorrigibly lazy. They are delighted when the plough breaks down, and immediately take a holiday with glee. They had just finished picking the crop, so were playing cricket, whilst three Whites employed about the place were hard at work. I was astonished at the extreme prominence of the supracilary ridges of the men's foreheads...and looks far more marked in the recent state than in the skull. The men were all dressed as Europeans and knew all about Mr WG Grace and the All-England Eleven...The great difficulty at these reserves is to manage the distribution of payment for labour. At present, all the proceeds went to a common stock. Of course, this makes all lazy.'

A race destroyed

A month later, on 7 April 1874, *Challenger* arrived at Sydney harbour at the mouth of the Hawkesbury River. Mosley went on an excursion inland to Berowra Creek, one of the many branches of the estuary into which the Hawkesbury River runs. He records numerous species of orchid, fern, the lyrebird, varieties of fish.

He continues, 'Beyond the extreme beauty of its wild and rocky scenery, the Browera Creek has yet another interest; it was in old times the haunt of numerous Aborigines, who lived on its banks in order to eat the oysters, mussels and fish.' He has come across numerous heaps of their discarded shells, a 'vast kitchen midden...so extensive that it has been a regular trade at which White men have worked all their lives, to turn over the heaps and sift out the undecomposed shells for making lime by burning them. Unfortunately, the numerous weapons thus found have been thrown away.'

'There is now not a single Black on the creek. Many of the middens are very ancient...the softer layers of the sandstone form numerous shelters and low roofed caves. The walls and roofs of the caves are covered all over with drawings executed by the blacks in charcoal on the rock.' He makes copies in his notebook of some of the drawings – a possum, a fish, and a white man, distinguished by the figure wearing a tall hat.

'Besides the drawings, in almost every cave were hand marks. These marks have been the subject of much discussion, and various speculations have been made as to some important meaning of the "Red Hand of Australia." These hand marks have been made by placing a hand against the flat stone, and then squirting a mixture of whitish clay and water from the mouth all around. The hand being removed, a tracing of it remains, and where the sandstone is red, appears red on a whitish background.'

Interestingly, he then observes: 'Delightful though it was at Sydney to make so many friends amongst one's own countrymen, after so long a voyage from home, one could not, as a naturalist, help feeling a lurking regret that matters were not still in the same condition as in the days of Captain Cook, and the colonists replaced by the race which they have ousted and destroyed, a race far more interesting and original from an anthropological point of view.'

European settlers including transported convicts arrived from 1788. In Sydney, including around Broken Bay and Berowra Creek, the devastating impact of social dislocation, disease, armed conflict and enforced dispossession came, almost immediately, with the colonisation of the area. For this reason, little first-hand information of the Sydney Aborigines has survived, much of the available knowledge filtered through the eyes of early colonists.

Berowra's local indigenous people were highly sophisticated, mobile hunter-gathers. A great diversity of resources were available seasonally, necessitating movement and trade between. There is evidence that Aborigines, principally the Garigal and Dharug peoples, were living in the Hawkesbury area for around 25,000 years before the Europeans arrived. The area around Berowra was the centre of Aboriginal spirituality for the Sydney region.

Berowra Creek was a meeting place where trade was regularly conducted between clans and tribes. Here, they would have fished, traded, found shelter and socialized together. Aboriginal artwork in carvings and cave paintings are found on either side of the creek. By 1795, much of the land was cleared to establish commercial farming, fertilised by lime from the shells left in the Aboriginal middens.

Meanwhile, when exploring in the wilds of the Queensland outback, Wyville Thomson discovered one of the most spectacular of the 'missing links' underpinning Darwin's theory of evolution: *Ceratodus*, or the lungfish. Spry records that Thomson returned to his laboratory 'laden with botanical wonders and fishing spoils', including 'several specimens of a peculiar fish called *Ceratodus*, or popularly, Barramundi.'

Ceratodus, the lungfish, has both lungs and gills, as well as rudimentary limbs for walking on land. *Challenger's* scientists were well aware of the importance of finding evidence of the vertebrates' sea-to-land transition. The idea that species change over time, give rise to new species, and share a common ancestor is at the heart of Darwin's theory of 'descent with modification.' The lungfish is part of a wider class of fish in the fossil record from which land-dwelling vertebrates evolved 300 million years ago. The Scientifics knew that their find of *Ceratodus* was hugely significant.

In Sydney harbour, while the ship was taken into the dry dock for repairs, the officers were making reparations for a 'grand Ball they are to give on shore this week to the people of Sydney. Two or three of our bandsmen are among the deserters,' Joe writes, 'so the band is rather demoralised just at present... Several of our men wish to leave the ship here as they don't like her, the work is too hard and the sea time so long, compared to other men-o-war in foreign stations…several men also to be invalided home as they are not able to stand the many sudden changes of climate experienced in this ship. We have lost nearly 30 since we came to Australia, & I am certain that if this had been any other ship then the *Challenger* I should have gone too…'

Challenger was made ready for the next stretch to New Zealand on 27 May. 'We shall lose more men before then,' Joe writes, 'and at New Zealand we shall lose some. Two got three months for trying to desert in Melbourne, & taking with them one of the ship's boats. Two more are awaiting court martial for deserting her, and two have been invalided. They are not the worst hands either that have gone since we came here and the Captain is in a great way about it. They are treating the men better now in hopes of deterring others from going, but the men only laugh. We have some great bullies and snobs among the officers & the work is much harder for everyone than it is in an ordinary man-o-war, and the pay is the same. There is not half the comfort in this ship that there was in the *Invincible* or *Audacious*. Our Issuing Room is a dog's hole … it is down below the water line & I have to do all my writing by candlelight going up to breath every two hours.'

On 8 June, *Challenger* left Sydney harbour still 25 hands short, although eight new hands were recruited as stokers, cooks, etc, and the imprisoned deserters were released back to the ship. Ahead lay an 1,180-mile eastbound voyage across the Tasman Sea to Wellington, surveying as she went the route for a telegraph cable to be laid between the two cities. 'We were to take a careful line of soundings across the shallow water,' Joe writes, 'for the cable is to be laid next year.'

The Pacific and Indian Oceans meet in the turbulent waters of the Tasman Sea, where heavy, rolling seas collide, making conditions rough and unpredictable. On Sunday 14 June, Joe writes, 'It blew very hard and was too rough for Church, but not for sounding, the Captain thought; so he sounded at 2,275 fathoms (about 2¾ miles).' The sea had deepened rapidly, and in hauling in the line, 1,500 fathoms were carried away, which the men attributed to 'sounding on the Sabbath and not having any surveying wine lately.' Campbell believed that there is 'no more abominable stretch of ocean as between Sydney and New Zealand. For the first few days we had nothing but gales and bad weather.'

Leadsman Edward Winton: 28 June 1874

On 28 June, as *Challenger* was approaching Wellington, the sea had been too rough for the crew to assemble on deck for prayers. The ship was cutting through shallower waters as she approached Wellington, so the leadsman, Edward Winton, took up his position out in the chains to swing the sounding lead into the heaving sea to test the depth. At 12 o'clock, all hands were piped to their dinner.

Joe writes, 'The officers then go to their lunch & all the rest of the ship's company to dinner, except for the Lieutenant in charge, the four men steering, the leadsman and the boatswain's Mate. The leadsman stands on a platform outside the ship to heave the lead. Just after the crew went to dinner the man sounding got his lead and line fouled round the anchor, and was seen by a marine to climb up to clear it.'

'Just at that time a frightful sea struck and broke over the fore port of the ship, shaking her from stem to stern. It capsized lots of plates and basins on the mess deck, but caused only a

Leadsmen standing in the chains, sounding the depth by lead and line.
Source: Eugène Pacini, La Marine: Arsenaux, Navires, Équipages, Navigation, Atterages, Combats, 1844.

general laugh. One facetious fellow said, "Who's that knocking on the door" and another told the sea to "Come in." But on the upper deck the sea had come and gone again, taking with it the poor leadsman from off the anchor, in all his thick winter clothing, sea boots and oilskins.'

'Then the ship righted herself again and went ploughing away for some ten minutes. The marine who saw the man go out to clear his line happened to look out to port and saw the line still round the anchor but no leadsman there. The Captain telegraphed the engine room to stop, all hands were called to put the ship about and in two minutes she was steaming fast back over the original track. Officers were aloft with glasses and nearly every soul on the ship was in the rigging looking out for some sign of him. A few minutes after, some dark object was seen right ahead and about a dozen men sang out, but on steaming up, it proved to be only seaweed and nothing more of the poor fellow was seen.'

'The deceased, Edward Winton, one of the finest and steadiest seamen on the ship, was about 25 years old, and married just before we left England. He was an excellent swimmer, but had on an enormous lot of clothes. We have just made a subscription on the lower deck for the widow of the poor fellow, & £20 was obtained from the crew alone, and I daresay the officers will raise another £30.'

Joe writes, 'He drowned in broad daylight whilst performing his duty, and not one of us to see him go, or throw him a life buoy. The ship went steaming on for Wellington and he to his last long home.'

As Spry remarks, 'The gloom which the loss of one of our small party occasioned was felt by everyone on board.'

The telegraph line between the two colonies was eventually completed in 1876. The cabling was manufactured at Samuel Silver's factory on the Thames. Over 12,500 miles of overland and undersea cable had already connected London to Adelaide. Contemporary accounts describe the completion of the London-Wellington link as the rubber-coated cable was hauled ashore: 'An event of the highest importance, in respect to the interests of intercolonial commerce.'

4

Pacific Ocean vast and wide

After a brief stopover in Wellington, *Challenger* headed north to begin a full two-year circuit of the Pacific Ocean. She stopped briefly at Tonga, Fiji and the New Hebrides, calling in for provisions at Cape York, the northernmost tip of Australia, in mid-September 1874. The settlement comprised but a half dozen houses left by a detachment of Royal Marines. The surrounding lands were of poor quality and the Colonial Government apparently faced 'frequent skirmishes with savage natives.' Spry went ashore. 'In my wanderings I came across some of the aborigines, houseless and homeless. They are poor, wretched specimens, the lowest in the scale of humanity; their dwellings, if such they can be called, being formed by a few bushes behind which they creep for shelter; dependent from day to day on what they can pick for food, not even having arrived at the simplest form of civilisation. I spent some time among them and gave them trifling presents, but could gain little information, for their intellectual capacities appeared very low.'

Challenger then sailed northwards for the low-lying Arafura archipelago, islands whose inhabitants were principally Papuan in origin. The naturalists went in search of birds of paradise.

While the photographer resumed his work of taking portraits of the islanders, a group of officers, including Campbell, took the steam pinnace and went exploring.

Here, again, Huxley's assertions of white superiority find expression in Lord Campbell's pen-portraits. 'I went into several huts,' he writes, 'all built on a number of slight bamboo or other supports, the roofs low-pitched, thatched, with projecting eaves…two or three steps up a broad bamboo ladder and we are in a Papuan home…in this hut there were seven or eight compartments, women and children in all of them, the former cooking or nursing babies. They asked us to sit. One or two of the young women were surprisingly good looking. Their hair is worn long, in a frizzly mop all around the head, or gathered back and tied in a loose chignon fashion. They wore nothing but the sarong or short matted kilts; they were very shy and very plump, these young women.'

'Their fires were burning on clay beds in movable boxes. The older men are ugly and very dark, wearing their hair in stiff, shaggy black mops or gathered back and tied like the women's. The bambinos were fat, naked littler animals and seemed well cared for. Overhead, resting across the light woodwork, were numbers of bows and arrows, ornamentally feathered with red and green parrot feathers…having nothing else in my pocket but a ten shilling gold piece, I offered it to a native for a fine set of bow and arrows, but he did not the least seem to know the meaning or value of gold, and refused.'

And later that day, coming down to the beach, 'I found two women getting into a canoe, and these certainly were very ugly and lean; hard work and no play makes these unfortunate women look very old.' A party of Papuan islanders were invited on board, guests of the captain and Wyville Thomson, where they were treated to refreshments and cigars. And Joe has no compunction in commenting that, 'they were the ugliest race of people we have yet seen, except the Aboriginals of Australia.'

On 16 December 1874, *Challenger* anchored in Hong Kong harbour among some 300 vessels of all nations and flags, including ten British men-of-war. Joe witnessed the devastation wrecked by a recent typhoon, which had overwhelmed the 'myriads of junks and sampans in which the floating population live and die.' The sea had risen many feet into the lower parts of the town, and 'two steamers are now lying one on top of the other close to the wharf, with their masts only above water.'

Yet Chinese traders immediately surrounded the ship: 'their bum boats had bread, all sorts of fruit, foreign butter and cheese, fried fish and prawns, & boiled and fried eggs. Every meal hour, these boats come alongside, and also do the other boats containing washerwomen, tailors, &c. Boats attend the ship day and night to take any one on shore who wishes to go. We often have geese for dinner in my mess, and sometimes a Chinese dinner from the shore of curried cats, dogs and sundries.'

While refitting the ship was underway, Captain Nares received a telegram commanding him to return home to lead a new Artic Expedition planned for the following spring. 'A new Captain has been appointed and will be here in 2 days, from Shanghai,' Joe writes. 'His name is Thomson, and he bears a bad name for tyranny on this station. He plays the fiddle and preaches his own sermons, but I will tell you more about him bye & bye.'

In town, Joe writes, he bought his father the gift of a new cane to replace the one Joe had accidentally broken. With regular shore leave now available, 'It is a very common occurrence to see 20 or 30 sedan chairs coming along the street, each containing a sailor with a cigar in his mouth & one foot out of each of the small windows. When they reach a public house they sing out "Shorten sail", keeping the chair waiting until they have had a good soaking. Very often they will meet an opposition party of American seamen when there is generally a squabble until the patrol comes and separates them. When there are no foreign sailors to fight with, our men fight each other.' Meanwhile, as Captain Frank Thurle Thomson settles into his new command, Joe observes that, 'he brought with him a piano, two fiddles, and his favourite tom cat.'

Earlier in his naval career, Captain George Nares had joined the search of the Arctic in 1852 for survivors of the ill-fated Franklin expedition. In 1845, Sir John Franklin, commanding the *Terror* and the *Erebus*, set out to discover the Northwest Passage, a fabled westward route linking the Atlantic Ocean with the Pacific Ocean through the unexplored furthest reaches of the Arctic Archipelago. But the two ships became locked in the ice and no trace of survivors was then found. After leading the British Arctic Expedition, Nares ended his career as a Vice-Admiral.

Before *Challenger* left Hong Kong, all the zoological and other specimens acquired since Sydney were landed and packed in over a hundred cases and several casks for transporting back to England. On 6 January 1875, after a refit and replenishment, *Challenger* left the crowded harbour to the accompaniment of much music from the British men-o-war anchored there. *Challenger's* course first took her northwards to New Guinea and across the Equator towards Japan.

Swire Deep: March 1875

Sub-Lieutenant Swire would enjoy one of his life's greatest achievements while leading the sounding operation off the Mariana Islands, midway between the Philippines and Japan. On 23 March 1875, Joe writes: 'This was a great day on board. At 6 am we sounded at the enormous depth of 4,600 fathoms. But as there was some doubt about it, the line was hauled up again, and sent down more heavily weighted & 2 patent Thermometers were attached. The depth was decided to be 4,550 fathoms (5⅙ miles), the greatest reliable depth ever obtained.'

Challenger's sounding weights had touched bottom at 27,000 feet. The temperature recorded was 34 degrees Fahrenheit on the sea bed and 80 degrees at the surface, although as a consequence of the great pressures at that depth, 'one of the Therm'trs burst owing to the tremendous pressure.' As Joe describes it, the sounding lead had fallen into 'some deep ocean valley almost as much below the surface of the sea as Mount Everest is above it.' To honour the occasion, and the popular young sub-lieutenant, the scientifics named the chasm the *Swire Deep*, although unfortunately for him the Royal Society later decided to rename it the *Challenger Deep*.

The abyss was by far the deepest part of the ocean floor *Challenger* surveyed. Modern echo sounding techniques of the Mariana Trench record a maximum depth at 38,000 feet, almost seven miles, the deepest part of any ocean. This chasm marks the dynamic interface between two downward moving tectonic plates in the north-east Pacific basin, the reverse of the upwelling zone that marks the Mid-Atlantic ridge.

On 11 April 1875, after a cruise of 3,000 miles, with no sail in sight for weeks on end, *Challenger* reached Tokyo Bay.

The following evening, Joe received a letter from his aunt informing him that his father had passed away. He wrote to his mother, 'I have heard of our great loss, but it seems hard to believe that Father has been buried nearly 4 months. I have not heard from you yet, nor from the boys, & I am anxious to know all the particulars. If there had been but a word of message from him, it would have seemed less hard to bear…I know by his manner that when he said good bye to me as I came away, he seemed to think it was for the last time.'

'By the time you get this we shall be "Homeward bound" & you will be able to count the months instead of the years as they fly by. I have fully determined to leave the navy when I get back. I shall have a little money and what is better, a *good character*! & hope we shall all be settled down in England & have many happy years yet in the old home!'

Challenger set sail from Yokohama on 16 June 1875, one year of the voyage remaining, 'with the homeward bound Pennant flying & the band playing Home Sweet Home as we steamed out past the other men-o-war.' Ahead lay the vastness of the Pacific Ocean, covering almost half of the Earth's surface. Midsummer found *Challenger* sailing and sounding almost daily on a track due east towards Hawaii. But the dredging hauls were poor, the seafloor in that region rocky and barren. It was a trying time for Herbert Swire: 'For nearly one mortal month we have been at sea without one sight of land and only once chancing across a ship. I am sick of it, so very much so.'

The expedition reached the Hawaiian archipelago on 27 July. A mail ship had arrived, but, Joe laments, there was 'not a single letter or newspaper for me from anyone; now I shall have to wait until we reach Valparaiso in November. I need not say how disappointed I am, for it is nearly a twelve month since

I heard from you or any of the boys…I scarcely know yet the particulars of poor father's death…If you have any bad news to tell, it is better to tell it at once than to leave people to "think and fear". I suppose I shall get a heavy mail in Valparaiso.'

Flowers in their hair: July 1875

But Honolulu offered frequent trips ashore. Joe finds the streets laid out exactly like an English town, with good horse roads. On weekdays, he writes, 'The men wear shirt & trousers & go bare-foot. The women wear a long coloured loose night gown, reaching to the ankles & generally no shoes and stockings, & their hair is worn either in two long plaits or hanging loose down the back. They wear natural flowers in their hair & also in their little straw hats. The principle amusements are bathing and horse riding.' All but the 'white ladies' ride astride their horse.

William Spry relates: 'Sometimes a crowd of these careless riders came galloping in from the plains full of laughter, accompanied by a lot of blue-jackets on leave from the *Challenger*, rushing helter-skelter, bestriding their horses as they would a topsail yard in a breeze; hanging on to manes and saddles, and enjoying themselves to their hearts content.'

Honolulu, *Challenger* Report.

Whilst strolling one evening, stopping to make a purchase, 'We saw a laughing, joking crowd of men and women; the latter clad in a single, bright coloured or white garment, falling free and in unconfined folds from the shoulder to the feet, while all wore wreaths of gorgeous flowers round their jaunty hats. These people are on the whole much better looking than those met with farther south. The nose is less flat, the lips are less prominent, the colour is a nearer approach to white, and the face altogether more indicative of intelligence and good nature, and they take more kindly to forms of European civilisation.'

Meanwhile, Moseley was listening to the 'most excellent musical band, numbering 20 or 30 performers, who executed complicated European music with accuracy and most pleasing effect.' On an excursion to Waimanalo, on the north-east side of the island, he collected a number of native skulls 'from a deserted burial place. The burials are amongst dunes of calcareous sand, and the bones exposed by the shifting of the sands by the wind...I know of no place where so abundant material is ready at hand for the study of the skeletal peculiarities of a savage race, by the examination of a long series of crania and skeletons, as are here. One, which was exhumed with care in situ, was buried with the knees bent up to the chest and the head bent forwards.'

On 19 August *Challenger* left Honolulu for the 2,400-mile journey to Tahiti, making 17 ocean soundings on the way. The dredge retrieved little more of importance than repeated hauls of red-brown clay and occasionally large quantities of black manganese ore. As *Challenger* approached the equator once more, Joe writes of the sudden death of one of the scientists, Dr Von Suhm, from a bacterial infection, erisypelas. The German-born naturalist had joined the ship at Sheerness, and, says Joe, was 'a fine healthy looking young man.'

Scientifics at work: HMS *Challenger* Report, Chapter 18.

Henry Moseley sat with him during the whole of the voyage, working day after day with the microscope at the same table. 'I am very greatly indebted to him for information on all branches of zoology,' he records, 'and leant very much from him in the way of method.' Von Suhm passed away on 13 September and was buried with naval honours, his body 'committed to the deep.'

Challenger reached Tahiti on 18 September 1875. On the approach to Papiete harbour, Joe says, 'I thought I had never seen such a beautiful place in all my life…the houses are all hidden by cocoa palms, bread fruit trees, orange trees, banana trees, and the great mountains rise just behind the town, their sides covered with vegetation, watered by numerous creeks, in which the natives seem to bathe and wash clothes the whole day…behind this island the sun sets every evening, painting the mountain every imaginable colour…The island seems made for the people, and the people seem made for the island.'

The bluejackets' band went ashore to play several times, while the crew were granted plenty of leave and spent a good deal of money in the town. Joe and some fellow sailors became acquainted with a group of English, French and Dutch settlers, whom they invited on board and to inspect the ship's albums 'containing photographs of all the countries and peoples we have visited.'

The chief engineer was beguiled: 'All shades of beauty were represented here, from swarthy Tahitian to the charming European; all however, dressed much alike, in long, loose, cool-looking drapery of all hues, shades and colours; their luxuriant tresses set off by brilliant flowers and masses of snowy reva-reva, a gauzy white material…it was pleasant to wander among the crowd, speaking freely and sociably, interchanging jokes or complements, or sitting down amongst a lot of lively native girls on their outspread mats…all generally so good-humoured that they could not fail to win one's esteem.'

And so, evidently, were the crew: 'This island & people have caused more desertions and punishments in the British Navy than all the rest of the islands of the Pacific together,' Joe claims. 'Captain Cook lost several men here, and it was on this island with the glimpse of a better life that the oppressed sailors on the Bounty resolved to mutiny. There are five men now in irons for swimming to shore & remaining all night; one man has deserted altogether and there are lots of leave breakers to be punished when we get to sea.'

Crusoe's island: November 1875

To the cry of 'Hands, up anchor,' *Challenger* pulled out of Tahiti's harbour on October 3 1875, serenaded by the local orchestra, her course eastbound towards the Chilean port of Valparaiso. Their next stopping place was Juan Fernandez, off the coast of Chile, the castaway island that inspired Daniel Defoe's *Robinson Crusoe* (1719). Ahead lay the Pacific Ocean vast and wide, a stage of more than 4,600 miles, with neither land nor vessel in sight for weeks on end.

On 'Crusoe's island': HMS *Challenger* Report.

'The voyage to Juan Fernandez occupied six weeks,' Herbert Swire retells, 'as we had the bad fortune to be becalmed for 12 days on the passage.' *Challenger* would lay awaiting a favourable breeze, or creep along at the rate of a sea mile an hour, for supplies of coal were insufficient to allow her to go under steam. Swire writes of officers' tempers fraying and faces turning sour in the wardroom.

But, finally, on 13 November 1875, *Challenger* reached Juan Fernandez' sheltered anchorage, Cumberland Bay, the breached crater of an old volcano ringed with precipitous cliffs save for the entry bar. Defoe's tale was based on the life of Alexander Selkirk, a Scottish seaman who, Joe explains in a letter, 'was left here in 1703 on account of some quarrel with his Captain.' The *Challenger* Report takes up his story: 'At first, Selkirk was much distressed by the want of bread and salt, but at length grew accustomed to do without them. Salt he might easily have procured had he wished, for the buccaneers in 1687 supplied themselves with that condiment by making salt pans near the seaside, and it is surprising that Selkirk did not follow their example. He soon wore out his shoes and clothes, and after a time, his feet became so hard that he felt no inconvenience from their absence. Goat skins furnished him with clothes, the pimento wood with fire by friction, and taming some kid goats with amusement.'

Selkirk was rescued from more than four years' isolation by a privateer, Captain Woodes Rogers. In his book, *Cruising Voyage round the World* (1719) Rogers describes his encounter with 'a man clothed in goat skins, who seemed wilder than the original owners of the apparel...and was sore distressed at being left alone in such a desolate place.' However, Defoe relocates his colonial tale to the West Indies. At the end of the story, Crusoe emerges a wealthy man, his riches accrued not from his own labours but from that of slaves on his plantation in Brazil.

Joe and other tars climbed up to the caves Selkirk supposedly inhabited. 'The largest is about 50 feet long,' Joe writes, 'the sides and roof are covered with beautiful green ferns and stalactites, which gives them a quite fairy-like appearance. Hundreds of English and American names are carved in their sides and I added mine to their number...The Captain issued wine to all hands, as this is the third anniversary of the *Challenger's* commission.'

Moseley made his way up to Selkirk's Monument, located at about 1,800 feet on the crest of a short, sharp ridge in a gap in the mountains. 'Here, Selkirk sat and watched the sea on both sides of the island in the long-deferred hope of sighting a sail. Juan Fernandez is only 20 square miles in area. Yet this tiny spot of land contains birds, land shells, trees and ferns which occur nowhere else in the vast expanse of the universe...Hovering over the flowering bushes and trees were everywhere to be seen two species of Humming Birds, one of which (*Eustephanus fernadensis*) is peculiar to the island…the male is very different in plumage from the female, being of a chocolate colour, with an iridescent golden brown patch on its head, whilst the female is green.' There was an abundance of ferns, of which Moseley identified twenty-four varieties.

The silence of five months without news broke on *Challenger's* arrival in Valparaiso, on 19 November 1875. 'I received 15 letters here,' Joe replies, 'some of which had been all round the world, and several papers… you do not say whether poor father received my last letter from Hong Kong or not…' As they entered the harbour, the band on board a French man-o-war struck up the tune of the Tahitian National Air, 'To greet us and recall,' Moseley reflects, 'the gaiety of the beautiful island we had left behind.'

5

Homeward Bound

On 11 December 1875, after a three week stopover in Valparaiso, *Challenger* set sail for the Magellan Straits on the tip of Patagonia, the crew buoyed by the prospect of making the Atlantic home run. *Challenger* had spent nearly two years circumnavigating the Pacific Ocean basin. Joe says, 'On Xmas eve we had a Concert which proved a great success and it is to be repeated once a fortnight…in addition to the ship's band there were Readings, recitations, dances and laughable Farces. The Captain played a very nice solo on the Violincello accompanied by several of the officers and scientific gents as well as the crew. After dinner there was dancing on the Main deck, and in the evening wine was issued to all hands. The Paymaster sent me a bottle of Madeira for my dinner.'

Moseley remarks that Mr Bird, the ship's bandmaster, 'has succeeded by his indefatigable efforts in training a very creditable brass band during the voyage, although only two or three at most of the bluejackets had any knowledge of music at all before the voyage commenced.'

At New Year, the captain and Wyville Thomson entertained officers and naturalists, and at midnight, sixteen bells rang the end of 1875. However, Joe says, 'the pleasantness only lasted until tea-time, for the seamen had managed to smuggle a great deal of liquor into the ship before leaving Valparaiso, which was brought out on Xmas night, and soon did its work, more than half of the crew were helplessly drunk and the quarrelling and fighting was something awful, and one poor fellow had his jaw broken in three places.'

To avoid the violent open seas around Cape Horn, *Challenger* made to weave her way slowly through the sheltered but tortuous islets and channels of the Magellan Straits, passing by barren shores beneath snow bound mountains. All aboard were now intent on her Atlantic home run. After a two-week stop-over on the Falkland Islands, *Challenger* crossed the Equator for the sixth and final time on 7 April 1876, in Longitude 14 degrees west, and steamed parallel with the African coast.

Approaching Cape Verde, Joe witnessed, 'One of the most wondrous sights I ever saw in my life, an enormous waterspout, said by our old hands to be the largest they had ever seen, like an enormous transparent factory chimney, its base resting on the sea and its apex hidden in a black cloud out of which lightening frequently flashed. The base of the column was in such violent commotion...dense volumes of water could be discerned ascending the column spirally until the wind caught it, when it was bent in the centre until it looked like the trunk of an old tree, very much bent, and breaking soon after.'

On 21 May 1876, *Challenger* took on her last 100 tons of coal at Vigo Bay on the coast of Spain, 'the hands working all night and finishing cleaning by 10 am.' Three days later, as *Challenger* reached home waters, 'Our band played *Homeward Bound* and *Auld Lang Syne* as we steamed through the fleet... We sighted old England when Start Point hove in sight about 15 miles north. Stood away up Channel under all possible sail and steam, the weather beautiful, cool and clear, there were more vessels passed during the day than we have seen since we left the Channel in December '72.' The traditional homeward bound pennant of rags, old trousers and cloths knotted together streamed out far behind, the full length of the ship and more.

The Scientifics disembarked as she rode anchor off Portsmouth, *Challenger* then continued up Channel until, on 27 May, the anchor was let go off Sheerness for the last time. 'The ship was full of visitors of all classes, and we discharged Powder and Shell,' Joe records. All hands went ashore to a thanksgiving service in the Dockyard church, after which leave was given to the ship's company. All the Deep Sea sounding, dredging and trawling apparatus was rigged for inspection by Vice Admiral Chadd, and the ship thrown open to the public. On Sunday 11 June, the ship was inspected by the Dockyard authorities, with savings bank money paid off at 11 am and wages due to the ship's company at 2 pm, when the crew was granted eight weeks' leave. 'Several of those who were entitled took their discharges from the Navy, myself among the number.'

Challenger's scientists regularly despatched their crates of zoological and botanical samples to the University of Edinburgh, where they were catalogued and sent for analysis to more than a hundred of the foremost specialists in their fields in Britain, Europe and North America. Some early findings were published in scientific journals before the *Challenger* returned to Portsmouth.

Birth of Oceanography

Professor Wyville Thomson began working on the official Expedition Report as soon as the scientists returned to their home institutions. Under his editorship, and then after his death from exhaustion, that of fellow scientist Sir John Murray, the final 50-volume Report was eventually readied for publication in 1895, the last chapter taking 20 years to complete.

As the expedition set off, Wyville Thomson had told the crew that the ocean deep was a 'sealed book to the human race.' Murray believed that the expedition's findings provided 'the greatest advance in the knowledge of our planet since the celebrated discoveries of the fifteenth and sixteenth centuries.' An era of global scientific cooperation began. The *Challenger Society for Marine Sciences* was founded in 1903, for the expedition had 'single-handedly founded the sciences that we know today as oceanography and marine geology.'

The expedition's collection of 4,772 specimens, details of which are available online, reveals an extraordinary cornucopia of marine life, including: sea snails from the Azores; squid from the waters around Japan; tiny filter-feeders dredged from more than 300 fathoms (550m) in the vicinity of the Hawaiian Islands; shark's teeth, crabs, 'sea pigs' (sea cucumbers) and snake eels. In first few months alone, the dredge retrieved a Venus Flower Basket (page 129), thought to be extinct, and the previously unknown 'manganese nodules'.

The ocean was no longer a 'sealed book', with the expedition's final reports extending to 30,000 pages, of which nearly 19,000 pages described marine specimens. Its finding established beyond doubt that there was no depth limit to animal life in the seas, even under conditions of extreme pressure and complete darkness.

Challenger's first great discovery was of the Mid-Atlantic Ridge, the 10,000 mile topographic rise dividing the Atlantic Ocean floor from the Arctic to the Cape of Good Hope. Revealed by volcanic peaks such as St Paul's Rocks rising from the ocean depths, the ridge marks the line of separation between the earth's great tectonic plates either side of the Atlantic Ocean.

The ship's surveys of the ocean floor paved the way for the expansion of the global submarine telegraph, notably the Sydney-Wellington link binding the Empire to London. And the growth of the extraordinary, satanic, cable manufacturing industries in Silvertown.

The great circulation patterns of ocean waters were gradually revealed by the expedition's painstaking measurements of ocean waters and their currents at over 500 observation stations in the open seas. The seas moved in discrete bodies with massive momentum about the globe. And from an analysis of the materials dredged up from the sea floor, which darkened in colour and content from chalky white in shallow seas to grey and then to deep red as the depth increased, they concluded that this was due to the increasing bleaching acidity of the oceans.

On their forays ashore, the naturalists had collected thousands of animal species that were often unknown. They observed and took samples of various plants and vegetation, both from the numerous islands visited and the longer inland excursions during the *Challenger's* four prolonged stopovers for refitting at Cape Town, Sydney, Hong Kong and Yokohama. As we have seen, in the Australian outback, Thomson recorded one of the most spectacular of the 'missing links' underpinning Darwin's theory of evolution: *Ceratodus*, the lungfish with lungs *and* gills, and rudimentary limbs for walking on land.

And on 23 March 1875, at a time when the bluejackets and officers alike were roundly tiring of the endless 'drudging,' *Challenger* sounded at the enormous depth of 4,600 fathoms, the greatest reliable depth ever sounded. The Mariana Trench marks the dynamic interface between the great tectonic plate of the Pacific Ocean's floor, which is sinking below the adjacent Philippine Plate, which carries the Mariana Islands.

The expedition's photographers took a thousand photographic plates, while numerous drawings and watercolours were made by the official artists, John Wild, and various officers and scientists.

At the conclusion of *Notes by a Naturalist*, Henry Moseley expresses his fear for the future of scientific exploration. 'It would be well to bear in mind,' he argues, 'that the deep sea, its physical features and its fauna, will remain for an indefinite period in the condition in which they now exist and as they have existed for ages past, with little or no change, to be investigated at leisure at any future time. On the surface of the earth, however, animals and plants and races of men are perishing rapidly day by day, and will be, like the Dodo, things of the past. The history of these things once gone can never be recovered, but must remain for ever a gap in the knowledge of mankind. The loss will be most deeply felt in the field of Anthropology, a science which is of higher importance to us than any other.'

Seabed samples retrieved and preserved by *Challenger* scientists are now stored in the Natural History Museum, London. But neither the deep sea nor its fauna 'will remain for an indefinite period in the condition in which they now exist,' as Moseley believed. For the thousands of ocean records and original dated and labelled glass jars now provide invaluable material to research the profound changes now taking place in the oceans and marine life, driven by climate change and ocean acidification.

Challenger sample jar,
Natural History Museum.

Race pseudo-science

One of the expedition's 50 reports was on *Human Skeletons: the Crania*, by Professor William Turner. He examined and tabulated 143 human skulls from 'aboriginal people, living in a state of uncivilisation,' collected by the *Challenger's* naturalists in Southern Africa, Southern America, Australia, and the islands of the Pacific Ocean. 'That they are uncultivated aborigines is a fact which should not be lost sight of in connection with this general summary of their characters,' Turner writes.

Drawing on the pseudo-science of the era, he drafted a 'classification of the various races of mankind' using a skull index combining the ratio of the length to the breadth of the skull with the relative amount of projection of the upper jaw.

He writes: 'From the examination of the *Races of Men* described in this Report, we have seen that in South Africa, in the southern part of South America, and in Australia, races of men exist distinguished by the small capacity of their crania, by their low intellectual development, and in the case of the Bushmen and Fuegians, by their small stature and generally feeble physical configuration. The Australians also, and the now extinct Tasmanians, were under the average size of Europeans. In the islands to the south and east of the great Asiatic continent the Andamanese and other Negrito tribes are distinguished by their small stature, microcephalic crania, and low state of intelligence.'

Such conjectures, perhaps better characterised as biological racism in this context, served to justify the so-called 'civilising' aims of British imperialism.

Half his life at sea

Challenger's voyage had covered 68,900 miles, the equivalent of almost three circumnavigations of the Earth, while burning 4,600 tons of coal despite using as much sail as possible. *Challenger's* hefty log books mark for every hour of every day her position, state of the weather and conditions of sail and steam. Her muster books provide a comprehensive tally of crew names and positions, pay, shore leave, accidents and fatalities. When she docked at Sheerness, only 144 of the original 230 crew remained. Joe reckoned that 60 sailors (a quarter of the crew) had deserted, while 11 had died, and 29 were invalided, discharged, imprisoned or exchanged.

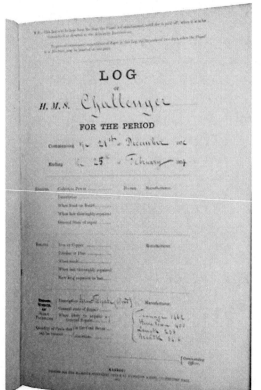

Challenger's log: 21 December 1872 to 25 February 1874.

Joe's final letter shows he had long set his mind on leaving the navy, 'finding sea life nought but vanity and vexation of the spirit, especially the latter.' In his final letter to his brother he quotes Dr Samuel Johnson: 'A ship is worse than a jail…When men come to like a sea-life, they are not fit to live on land.'

Engineer Spry closed his diary with warmer thoughts of the ties that had bound the crew together: 'All those close associations will be severed and each one of the *Challenger's* crew goes his way, to seek relaxation and pleasure amongst home scenes and friends near and dear to him.'

The muster book shows that Joe Matkin, the Ship's Stewards Assist (named 'George Matkin' in the ledger), was 'Paid off' with £73 and discharged to shore, with a 'Good conduct' record.

The book also shows that Charles Collings disembarked with three payments worth £146 all told. Alongside his name is his seaman's number (64774), and rank (2B) marking that

HMS *Challenger* muster book, April-June 1876:
Entries for Charles Collings and George (Joe) Matkin.

he enlisted as a Sailor Boy 2nd Class. He was made up to Seaman (SM) on 10 August 1866, aged 18 years. Charlie left the service with a 'V Good' conduct record, and was discharged from navy service after a few weeks on HMS *Pembroke* on his twenty-eighth birthday, 28 August 1876.

Charlie Collings had spent half of his twenty-eight years, and most of his marriage so far at sea. The *Challenger* expedition was to leave an enduring mark on his life.

Challenger was re-commissioned as a Coast Guard and Royal Naval Reserve training ship at Harwich, and she remained in reserve until she was broken up and sold for her copper bottom in 1921. Her figurehead is kept at the National Oceanography Centre, Southampton.

Challenger decommissioned, *Challenger* Report, chapter 21.

- Part Three -

The Sea Never Let Him Go

I have two photographs of my great grandfather. The first, as we have seen, captures the moment when a group of sailors from HMS *Challenger* came to the rescue of the Stoltenhoff brothers, marooned on Inaccessible Island in the South Atlantic. Leading Stoker Collings is in the back row third from the left, behind taller men, with a thick, dark beard, serious face, a sailor's cap angled above a broad forehead. All stand on the grassy shore in front of the brothers' thatched hut. The photo was taken in October 1873, when he was 27 years old. It's one of more than a thousand images in the expedition's official archives, and a rare one of the sailors themselves.

In the second, a studio photograph, taken some forty years later, around 1910, Charlie is wearing a respectable suit with a high-buttoned waistcoat, collar and tie. There is something firm and solid about his build. He is profiled side on, with a long pointed nose and receding hair. The bushy beard is replaced by long side whiskers. The gaze is firm, with perhaps the hint of a smile. The accompanying studio photo of Mary, probably taken at the same time, shows her straight-backed, wearing a two-tone, high waisted dress, with her hair tidied back into a beaded snood, or net.

Charlie Collins (1847-1932) and his wife, Mary Collins (1850 – 1918).

My mother had once said of her grandfather, 'He sailed on the *Challenger*, on the Nares-Thomson expedition to the South Pole. There used to be a picture of the ship once. He'd been to China, too, on the Cutty Sark. And when he came back to settle, he would enjoy his whisky and kept a bottle in the wardrobe in his bedroom.'

Raised by the sea

AUGUST 1847

Charlie was born on 19 August 1847 and baptised Charles
Matthew Collings. His mother, Caroline Collings, was an
unmarried twenty-year-old, living with her parents at 28 Kemp
Street, Brighton. His father is not named on the baptism certif-
icate. The following year, on 17 July 1848, Caroline married
Charles Napoleon Matthewman in St Nicholas Church,
Brighton. The marriage certificate, recording the occupations
of male relatives, states that her husband was a plasterer, her
father a bricklayer, and her father-in-law a surgeon. In fact,
Caroline worked as a laundress.

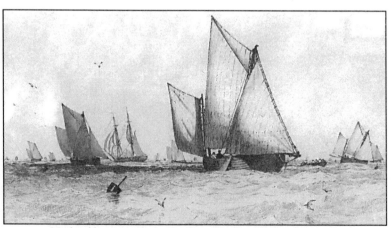

Mackerel boats coming in, Brighton (Brighton Fishing Museum).

In Charlie's childhood, Brighton had the largest fishing fleet on the Sussex coast, comprising over fifty large sea boats. In the autumn, the forty-foot luggers would go after the herring with drift nets, starting on the east coast of Scotland, coming down south to Scarborough and Yarmouth, and returning to Brighton at Christmas. In the New Year, the same boats would set off to Land's End and chase the mackerel along the English Channel. The boats were winched up the shingle beaches between the Palace and West Piers and down by Black Rock, beneath the narrow streets where Charlie was brought up. Here, they would unload and sell their catches off flatback barrows. In the summer, boats such as *The Skylark*, would offer holidaymakers 'a lovely ride out.'

Charlie had twelve brothers and sisters. After he left school, Charlie initially followed his father's trade as a plasterer, as did some of his younger brothers. The 1861 Census shows the thirteen-year-old had left Brighton and moved along the coast to live in board and lodgings with his father at 12, Alfred Street, Hastings. They are both named in the census as Charles Matthewman; his father's occupation is described as a plasterer, Charlie is a plasterer labourer.

A single minded boy

1 January 1863

But Charlie had clearly resolved to join the Royal Navy. According to my aunt, Stella Hale, 'Old Grandad Collins, Charles Matthewman Collings, ran away from his family without his family's sanction, and he took his mother's surname, Collings.' My mother believed he was also unwilling to reveal his father's middle name, Napoleon.

On New Year's Day 1863, single minded, he enlisted under the name Charles Collings. His uncle, Henry Collings, accompanied the boy to Portsmouth that day as they went through the Navy's recruitment process. The paperwork shows that Henry provided 'parental' consent: 'This is to certify that my son, Charles Collings, has my full consent (himself willing) to enter Her Majesty's Navy for a period of Ten Years Continuous General Service from the age of 18, in addition to whatever period may be necessary to attain that age.'

In effect, he was committing to 14 years' naval service. Charlie's signature appears to be in his uncle's hand. The date of birth, August 1848, is also incorrect; he was a year older. Perhaps Charlie believed he was born the year his parents married.

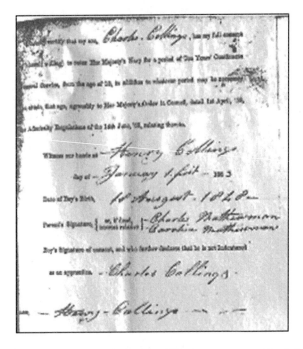

The recruitment form describes Charlie as having 'dark brown hair, hazel eyes, a dark brown complexion, no other distinguishing marks, 5 feet and ¼ inch tall, Brighton born.' Passing the navy's standard admission test, he is described as, 'Well grown, stout, perfectly sound and healthy constitution, free from all physical malformation and intelligent.'

Now enlisted as a Boy Sailor, 2nd Class, Charlie was sent off to the training ship, HMS *St Vincent*, one of the hulks lying at Portsmouth docks, where he spent his first year with hundreds of other trainees learning seamen's skills. A sense of what that first year in the navy was like can be drawn from the accounts of two of his near-contemporaries on the *St Vincent*, Thomas Holman and Charles Humphreys. In *Before the Mast*, they describe the routines drilled into them as boy recruits.

No. 95.

1863

Boys enter for Continuous Service, (C.S.) Commanding Officers are immediately to fill up this Form and transmit it to the Accountant General of the Navy.

and Surname in full .... **Charles Collings**

Born.—[If born out of Her Majesty's Dominions, it must be stated whether the parents are British Subjects. Foreigners not being allowed to volunteer for Continuous Service.]

Brighton Sussex

of Birth.—[Great care is to be taken that the date is correctly stated.]

18 August 18**48**

tion ....

Height **5. 0 ¼** Complexion **Dark**

Hair **Dk Brown** Eyes **Hazel**

Marks **None**

which he entered .... **St Vincent**

of Entry in Do. .... **1 January 1863**

g in Do. .... **Boy 2nd Class.**

Volunteering for Continuous Service.... **18 August 1866**

for which he Volunteered .... **10 Years.**

of Badges ....

Certificates, or Class, as Seaman Gunner..

ent of all former Service in the Navy, ther as Seaman or Boy, with names of and dates of Entry and Discharge; and Men have also served in Dockyards, guard, or Revenue Vessels, the names he Dockyards, Coastguard Stations, and enue Vessels, with period of Service, to be d.

First Entry.

[See over.

Catalogue Reference:ADM/139/549   Image Reference:

Thomas Holman's day started with reveille at 5.30 am, with the bosun's call to Rouse up, with a voice 'at least three notes below the bellow of a bull,' Holman says. Half the boys swabbed decks until 6.30 am, the rest cleared the mess deck. A swim followed for those who could.

Breakfast was at 7.15 am, followed by sail drills between 8 am and 9 am. All recruits then assembled on deck for morning prayers, with more seamanship to follow: 'swimming, boat pulling, knots and splices, monkey topsail yard.' Before they were let loose aloft among the high spars, the boys were taught to loosen and furl the sails by standing on a spar at deck level. Next came drills on 'the ship, compass, helm and lead, and gun, rifle and cutlass.' Dinner was at 12 noon, their only hot meal of the day.

Boy Sailors on the *St Vincent*

At 1 pm, an assembly on the main deck marked the start of the afternoon's instruction. At 3 pm, clothes were washed and hung out. The boys had tea at 5 pm, followed by more deck washing this time on the upper deck. Finally, the boys had free time until hammocks were 'piped down' at 8.30 pm. Lights were extinguished at 9 pm, 'after which silence should prevail, but seldom did.'

After breakfast on Sundays, Thomas Holman says, 'We dressed in our very best and cleanest to go on decks…Church was followed by the best dinner of the week, and a run ashore.' The Boys also had Thursday afternoons ashore, and entertainments and singing on Saturday evenings. Holman remembers: 'The weeks floated past, and I felt myself becoming more and more a sailor boy.'

However, young Charles Humphreys, who arrived on the *St Vincent* in November 1870, says, 'I cannot describe those 12 months of learning discipline. We were very often short of food and many a rope's end did I feel. Our instructors were very cruel… At midsummer, those who had homes and parents who could afford it, were allowed to go home for three weeks. Those who stayed behind had to clean the ship and do other work…Being a long way from home and my parents very poor, I had to remain on board.'

For his part, Charlie was a willing volunteer, unlike many of the lads who joined the navy at that time, very often orphans with no home to go to, sent for navy service by the Marine Society, or some other charitable institution. Charlie would have returned home to Brighton for his first few weeks' shore leave in midsummer, 1863.

Stoker

Charlie qualified as an Able Seaman on 18 August 1866, aged 18, so beginning a mandatory ten years of continuous service. His record papers show that he was by now a blacksmith by trade, instructed in the navy's workshops on Portsmouth Docks in the skills to mend or newly forge the blocks, chains and other parts of a ship's metalwork. The trade also opened up the possibility of better paid work as a stoker. Now an Able Seaman, a new 'Personal Description' reveals that he had grown by three inches to 5 feet 3 ½ inches tall, with 'dark brown hair', and a 'sallow' complexion. His 'wounds, scars or marks' included tattoos of a 'ship on breast', 'crucifix on right arm', an 'Eurydice on left arm' and 'bracelets on wrists.'

Each tattoo tells a story. A fully-rigged ship signifies that a sailor had rounded Cape Horn. The tattoo of a cross symbolises hope, or salvation. And an 'Eurydice,' or sea nymph, was a figure in Greek mythology, the wife whom Orpheus the voyager brought back from the dead with his enchanting music. Such details were required for identification in the event of injury, death or a pension claim. His service record also shows he was awarded a Good Conduct Badge (one stripe of gold lace) in 1872 or 1874, worth an extra penny a day on his pay.

With blacksmith's skills and the lure of better pay, Charlie enlisted as a stoker on HMS *Penelope*, which undertook coastal patrol duties in home waters. A stoker's work was arduous. According to Chamberlain's *Social History of Royal Navy Stokers*, most seamen would not have swapped the dire discomforts of keeping watch on the upper-deck in midwinter for the dust laden air, heat, noise and physical labour of the stokehole, not even for a stoker's higher wages. Long before the effects of exposure to coal dust and asbestos were understood, stokers endured the daily rigours of hard physical work conducted under conditions which could result in scalds from steam bursts, burns, injuries, cramps from dehydration, or heat exhaustion. Apparently, the old stoker's practice of keeping a piece of coal in the mouth while in the stokehole was still prevalent in Charlie's day. The practice, it was claimed, would help to maintain a gentle flow of saliva, avoiding the need for stokers to continually drink water.

A whirlwind romance

May 1870

One family legend has it that Charlie proposed to Mary Francis Patching after a 'whirlwind Cornish romance.' Perhaps they met when he was on shore leave in Devonport, south Devon. Be that as it may, they were married on Sunday 15 May 1870 at the 12th century parish church of St Bartholomew in the village of Maresfield, Sussex. HMS *Penelope's* muster book records Charlie's two weeks' leave, from 13 to 30 May, while it anchored off the Kent coast at Deal. He was a 23-year-old stoker, she was twenty years old, and although again her occupation isn't recorded on the marriage certificate, she lived and worked at the laundry House at Reedings Farm, on the edge of the village.

The two witnesses to the ceremony were John Mercer (Mary's older half-brother by her mother's first marriage), and Mary Ann Matthewman (Charlie's sister). On the marriage certificate, the bride's father is given as George Patching (a bailiff), while the groom's is said to be Charles Collins (plasterer), but this is incorrect; it seems likely that Charlie's father did not attend the wedding.

After the ceremony, on leaving the square towered church in a peal of bells, they would have made their way eventually down

St Bartholomew's Church, Maresfield, Sussex.

Nursery Lane to Reedings Farm, passing between maytime hedgerows veil-hung with white blossoms of hawthorn and heady scented elder flowers. A mile out of town they would reach their marital home to be, the Laundry House. Recently, Mary and her elderly mother, Ann Patching, had left Brighton to take over the laundry business and set up home there. In the 1871 Census, their seven-member household comprises Ann, her two daughters, two grandchildren and a domestic servant.

1871 Census: Reedings Farm, Maresfield

Name	Age	Year born	Relation	Occupation
Ann Patching	62	1809	Head	Laundress Mistress
Mary Collins	21	1850	Daughter	Assistant Laundress
Elizabeth Dowsett	29	1842	Daughter	Agricultural Labourer
Elizabeth Dowsett	5	1866	Grand daughter	Scholar
George Dowsett	2	1869	Grandson	Scholar
Emily Mitchell	14	1857	Servant	Domestic Servant
James Henry Dowsett	6m	1871	Grandson	

Ann was the laundry mistress and Mary her assistant. This was a time when in every town and village women were working at small hand laundries, where the work to wash, starch and iron was hard, physical and skilful, the hours long, the working conditions hot and damp, and the wages low.

Charlie returned from his fortnight's leave to stoking duties on *Penelope*, a steam and sail armoured corvette on coastal patrol in the English Channel. Sometimes she would lie at anchor in the quiet bay off Deal on the Kent coast, or re-provision at Harwich docks, so that during the first year of their marriage, as *Penelope's* muster book reveals, stoker Collins squirrelled leave for an occasional day or two at home.

Just over a year after they were married, Mary's first child, Charles John George Collins, was born on 11 June 1871, at the Laundry House, Maresfield. Charlie would have received news of the birth while on board *Penelope*. The muster book shows he took four days' leave at the end of June 1871, most likely

HMS *Penelope*.

when he was to greet his son for the first time. He returned again on leave in September, 1871. Yet that handful of days, marked in *Penelope's* leave register, were probably the only times they were able to spend at home together as a family, for their infant son, John, died on 25 October 1871. Mary alone would have laid the boy to rest in the graveyard of St Bartholomew's church. His father was back at sea. There was to be no more home leave for Charlie until December 1871.

Challenger crewman

NOVEMBER 1872

A year after their bereavement, Charlie opted to change ships, from *Penelope* to *Crocodile*, and then on 15 November 1872 he volunteered for the *Challenger* expedition. The ship was under the overall command of Arctic explorer Captain George Nares, with its scientific work led by Professor Wyville Thomson. The first of the *Challenger's* muster books (November-December 1872) names all of the expedition's crew of 230 bluejackets, marines, officers and scientists. Charlie is among the men in the 'Steam Department,' including eleven stokers, three coal trimmers and four leading stokers, of whom 'Charles Collings' was the senior and highest paid, earning £5.9s.8d a month (£65 10s a year), and with two service badges to his name. He was earning roughly twice the annual wage of a standard able seaman at the time. A leading stoker was more highly valued than a standard Able Seaman, having considerably more responsibility but working in even tougher conditions.

Challenger sailed from Portsmouth in December 1872, on a four-year voyage that was to cover over 67,000 miles. As my mother recalled, 'Charlie sailed on the *Challenger*, on the Nares-Thomson expedition to the South Pole.' *Challenger* wasn't equipped for a Polar expedition, although she did cross the Antarctic Circle and penetrate the Great Antarctic Ice Barrier. None of Charlie's letters home survive, yet thanks to my distant relative, Emma Collins, there's that saved image of him on Inaccessible Island. Meanwhile, the letters of his shipmate, Joe Matkin, recently published in *At Sea with the Scientifics* (1992), provide the only sailor's narrative of the expedition, pieced together from 69 of Joe's letters home.

Both Charlie and Joe left the navy when the ship returned to Sheerness Dock on the Thames estuary in May 1876, at the end of their ten years' mandatory continuous service. Charlie returned home to Maresfield and his wife Mary Francis, with a blacksmith's skills and almost three years' pay in his pocket. Joe rejoined his printing family in Rutland and then went on to a life as a Whitehall civil servant.

Swallowing the anchor

1876

Charlie left the service, 'swallowing the anchor,' as it was called. He changed his surname from Collings to Collins for good, and with Mary, his wife of six years, returned to live in Brighton for a domestic life he had never really known. With the help of their savings, the couple first of all took a licence to manage the Golden Cross, a beer house at 103, North Road, Brighton, where their second child, George, was born in 1879.

Later that year the family moved to 46, Viaduct Road, Brighton, a two-storey terraced house, where they managed a general store. The 1881 Census records that Mary's elderly mother, Mary Patching, was also living with them, as well as three young apprentice engineers. Street directories show Charlie's various occupations during the twenty years they lived at Viaduct Road included 'storekeeper, ironmonger, bell hanger and gas fitter.' At one time, according to my aunty Edith, he was contracted to install a new set of iron railings at the Court Theatre, adjacent to the Royal Pavilion, Brighton.

It can never have been easy for Charlie to go sailing no more. My mother once said, 'At times they were quite well off, and at others he'd be selling fish round the market while his wife would be taking in washing.' His renowned 'disappearances,' perhaps on the drink or back on a ship, would leave Mary to

1881 Census: 47 Viaduct Road, Brighton.

Name	Age	Year born	Relation	Occupation
Charles Collins	34	1847	Head	Store Keeper, Shop
Mary F Collins	31	1850	Wife	
George A Collins	1	1880	Son	
Mary A Patching	72	1809	Mother in law	Annuitant
Henry Cooke	19	1862	Lodger	Engine Fitter
Thomas Lee	20	1861	Lodger	Engine Fitter Apprentice
Henry Lee	19	1862	Lodger	Engine Fitter Apprentice

fend for their offspring. Mary, a laundress and hardworking, intelligent woman, bore them nine children altogether: John, George, Alfred, John, Ernest, Annie, Elizabeth, Charles and Albert. Three of her children (the two Johns and Albert) died in their infancy. According to my mother, their second John died of diphtheria in 1887, at two years of age. At that time, children under five were particularly at risk from the contagious bacterial infection.

During the Great War, Charlie and Mary, now both in their mid-sixties, moved in with their eldest son, George, his wife, Edith May, and their three children (Edith, George and Stella), at 47, Springfield Road, Brighton, a three-storey bay windowed house. My mother, Stella, the youngest of the three, was born there in 1915.

Her father, whom we all affectionately knew as 'Pop,' had closed up his mechanical engineering business in 1916 to join the war effort as a Royal Navy submariner. The submarine's engines failed whilst on active service in the North Sea, leaving it stranded on the seabed. All were feared lost. For three days, whilst working to repair the engines, Pop was inhaling gases released from the battery acids. The submarine then resurfaced. He spent long months of convalescence in a nursing home in Kent, and was invalided out of the service in 1919.

Edith May Collins, with Edith, George and Stella: 1915.

After the war he first managed a touring mobile electric cinema with shows across the towns and villages of Sussex and Kent. He then opened an engineering workshop and petrol filling station on the London Road into Brighton. Pop was a church organist, played piano in a trio, gave his grandchildren maths and music lessons, never wore socks, and was a lifelong teetotaler.

'Pop' – George Collins, 1916.

An exceptional woman

June 1918

Mary passed away at Springfield Road in June 1918, aged 68. A coroner's report was required because there was no doctor present at her passing. The record shows that she died of a stroke while being cared for by her daughter-in-law, Edith May. My mother, Stella, once said: 'My Mum was very fond of Mary. She was very intelligent. When grandad would disappear, she used to take in washing. She had a mangle, and a horse and cart to fetch and deliver laundry. She sent all her children to a fee-paying school at the bottom of Ditchling Road, which gave them a better start. She bought my Pop a piano and paid for his lessons, as he was very fond of music.'

My mother was too young to remember her, but she and her siblings, George and Edith, shared the house with their grandfather for much of the time until he died in 1932. The Springfield Hotel was a few yards from the house, by London Road station and a row of shops. My mother recalls: 'Charlie would go up the road to the local pub with his cronies, who were also Irish, and they'd sit and talk of dear old Ireland, and how much they missed it. Then he would come home and call them a load of old hypocrites who had no intention of returning to Ireland.'

'George and me used to play outside the pub and sometimes we would put our heads round the door. "Grandad, grandad," we would say, "can we have some lemonade, grandad?" "Hello my pretties," he would say, "Hello my pretties," the devoted grandfather in front of his pals. He would buy us a lemonade and take it outside, and then say, "Here's your lemonade. Now bugger off!"'

My mother's older sister, Edith, remembers: 'His wife, Mary, came from a quite well-off family, but they refused to keep giving her money when Grandad Collins went on his binges. This was after he retired from the navy. Their circumstances seemed to go up and down in time with his drinking bouts. He worked for a building firm, J.J. Saunders. He was a skilled worker.'

'There is the story about the vicar of Preston, who used to come to their house in Springfield Road for a bath. Being a builder, Grandad Collins had ensured that his was one of the first houses to have a bathroom. But Grandad Collins learned that the vicar had taken on someone else to carry out some building work on the vicarage. The next time the vicar arrived for his bath he was sent packing. He was that angry he was wielding an axe as the man came to the door.'

When Charlie was in his early eighties he moved across town to live with his daughters, Annie and Netty, at 7 Atlingworth Street, Kemp Town. The sisters' tall, bay windowed, terraced house, The Anchorage, had a sea view from the front rooms. They ran it as a boarding house for the elderly and infirm.

My aunt, Stella Phyllis Hale, was fostered into Annie's care as a young child and eventually adopted by them. She recalls, 'Grandad, Charlie Collins, was living with us in Atlingworth Street. There was a picture of HMS *Challenger* in the living room, a black and white drawing. I understood that old Grandad Collins, Charles Matthewman Collins, ran away from his family without his family's sanction, and took his mother's surname of Collings.'

My aunt's mother, Irene Key, a friend of Annie's, emigrated to America but never kept her promise to send for her daughter. Letters would come from Boston enclosing small denominations of dollar bills towards Stella's upkeep. But the money stopped coming, and in a final letter she beseeches Annie to take care of her daughter. After that, my aunt was made to work for her keep, even as a child. The boarding house accommodated eleven elderly residents, including Charlie. All before school, she would have to clean the hearth stones and wash down the front steps, lay out clean cutlery, lay fires and make and serve the residents' porridge in their rooms. 'Once, when I was ill with pneumonia, I remember being in a steam tent, and he would go out for strawberries for me. He could have been Mayor of Brighton. But when he was drunk he'd go around the streets crying out, "Mackerel, bloody fine mackerel."'

Veteran sailor passes

Charlie passed away at Atlingworth Street on 29 September 1932, aged 85. According to the death certificate, he apparently died of 'apoplexy and senility.' His daughter, Annie, registered her late father's trade as 'ex-whitesmith,' denoting the craft of a skilled metalworker undertaking the finishing of iron and steel products: filing, lathing, burnishing, fitting, and bellhanging. But press reports describe him as the 'last survivor of the Nares-Thomson scientific expedition on HMS *Challenger*. One of the most gigantic undertakings of its kind.'

'When grandfather died,' my mother recalls, 'there was a grand funeral through the town, with the Union Jack draped on the coffin, for he was one of the last surviving members of that crew. Uncle George wore a short stove pipe hat, and it kept falling down over his eyes, only his nose stopped his face from disappearing altogether into this shiny black tube. The children were laughing when we should have been sober, riding along in a horse drawn open carriage with the rest of the family. The four black horses pulling the hearse wore plumes.'

And so, on Sunday 2 October 1932, following the procession through town, Charlie was buried with Naval honours, alongside his late wife, Mary, in Brighton cemetery, high on a hillside with a view of the English Channel to the west, and the setting sun.

Thanks to his long life, their grandchildren - Stella, Edith and George, and by adoption, Stella Phyllis – were to give us a sense of this restless seafarer and his wife, Mary.

A VETERAN SAILOR PASSES

FUNERAL OF MR. CHARLES COLLINS

Believed to be the 'last survivor of the Nares-Thompson scientific expedition in H.M.S. "Challenger" in 1872, Mr. Charles Collins, of 7 Aliingworth-street, Brighton, was laid to rest in the Brighton Borough Cemetery on Tuesday afternoon.

Mr. Collins joined the Navy when a lad of 14, and retired at the termination of the great expedition in 1876. This expedition, which was organized by the Government, was one of the most gigantic undertakings of its kind. Its purpose was to gain information concerning chemical, bacteriological and biological research work in the great oceans, also soundings of sea beds, depths of the ocean and underseas currents. It was grim pioneer work from first to last.

The "Challenger" left England in November, 1872, and returned in May, 1876. The total distance travelled was 68,784 miles and the total time away was three years, 167 days. Many of the leading professors of the day were on board, and those in com-

was 68,784 miles and the total time away was three years, 167 days. Many of the leading professors of the day were on board, and those in command were Captain G. S. Nares and Captain F. T. Thompson.

After His Retirement

Mr. Collins, as a member of the crew, had a lot to do with the care of the engines. On his retirement from the Navy he came to live in Brighton and started a business in Viaduct-road. He was for many years employed by Messrs. J. J. G. Saunders and Sons, builders, of Brighton. When he left this firm he retired and lived with his sons and daughters for some years. He was responsible for the iron work of the old Court Theatre in New-road and other buildings in Brighton.

Mr. Collins passed away just past five bells in the evening watch of 29th September. He was in his 85th year.

A Private Funeral

The funeral, which was private and without mourning, was attended by the relatives of Mr. Collins and one friend. The service was held at St. Mary's Church and was conducted by the Vicar, the Rev. George A. C. Smith-Cranmoor. Father Bates, of St. Martin's Church, was also at the cemetery.

The mourners were Charles, George and Alfred (sons); Edith, Annie and Elizabeth (daughters), Edie, George, Bert, Stella, Dorothy and Stella Phyllis (grandchildren), Mrs. Purdy, Mrs. Amrey and Mrs. Chappell (sisters), Rhoda and Elizabeth (daughters-in-law), Mr. S. Chappell (brother-in-law), Mr. Ellis Banfield (a very old friend) and many others. There were many lovely flowers. The coffin was draped with the Union Jack.

Mr. Collins was laid to rest by the side of his wife.

A BRIGHTON NAVAL VETERAN

COVERED WITH THE UNION JACK, the coffin bearing the remains of Mr. Charles Collins, last member of the ship's company of The Nares-Thompson Scientific Expedition in H.M.S. "Challenger" (1872-6), whose burial took place yesterday Brighton Borough Cemetery.

Charlie and Mary Collins
A family tree

Charles Napoleon Matthewman (1821-1906) & Caroline Collings (1827-1901)
Married 1848

Charles Matthew Collings (1847-1932); and Mary, Henry, James, David, Caroline, Albert, Sarah, Elizabeth, Jane, Agnes, Eleanor and Kate Matthewman

∞∞∞∞∞∞∞∞∞∞∞∞∞∞∞∞∞∞∞∞∞∞∞∞∞∞∞∞∞∞∞∞∞

Charles Matthew Collin(g)s & Mary Francis Patching
Married August 1870

Charles John Collings (June-October 1871)   Edith Anne (1888-1954)

George (1879-1961)   Elizabeth (1889-1939)

Alfred (1882 -1966)   Charles (1891-1954) and

John (1885-1887)   Albert Collins (1895-1900)

Ernest (1887-1959)

∞∞∞∞∞∞∞∞∞∞∞∞∞∞∞∞∞∞∞∞∞∞∞∞∞∞∞∞∞∞∞∞∞

George Collins & Edith May Dapp (1881-1932)

Married November 1900

Edith (1907-2008)   George (1912-1985)   Stella Dorothy (1915-1982)

....

Edith Anne Collins

Adopted

Stella Phyllis Hale (1915-2008)

∞∞∞∞∞∞∞∞∞∞∞∞∞∞∞∞∞∞∞∞∞∞∞∞∞∞∞∞∞∞∞∞∞

Stella Dorothy Collins (1915-1982) & Gordon Pearson (1917-1981)

Married June 1940

Gillian   Philip   Suzanne   Paul

Acknowledgements

This book was inspired by the often-told stories and memories of my great-grandfather, Charlie, and his wife, Mary, for their grandchildren remembered them well: my mother, Stella Pearson née Collins, her siblings Edith and George and their adopted cousin Stella Phyllis Hale. I am also grateful to a distant relative, Emma Collins, for her blog about Charlie on My Brighton and Hove, a local history website:

www.mybrightonandhove.org.uk/page/charles_matthewman_collins_around_the_world_in_713_days

George's son (my cousin Tony), and his wife Diana generously shared their family researches. I retraced their steps through newspaper and other archives, finding contemporary accounts of Charlie's life and times, and a photo of Charlie's funeral in the Sussex Daily News.

My grateful thanks to Angela Colling, editor of the *Challenger* Society's magazine, Ocean Challenge, and Louisa Watts, John Phillips and Tony Rice of the *Challenger* Society for invaluable advice and insights about the *Challenger* Expedition. However, any errors or omissions in this account are entirely my own. The magazine published my note about Charlie in *A song for the Challenger's crew* in the organisation's journal, Vol. 23, No.2, (2019): www.challenger-society.org.uk/oceanchallenge/2019_23_2.pdf

My thanks to Andrea Watts, inspirational tutor at the Mary Ward Centre's Life Writing class, where many first ideas were explored, and to my classmates, Anne Job, Pat Mary Brown and Rocio Vasquez for their constant support.

I am hugely grateful to my ever-patient literary editor, Caroline Gilfillan, and to Mick Shew, Sue Wilsea, Heather De Lyon, Alison Whyte and Francesca Klug for their comments on earlier drafts. My thanks to Nick Grant for crafting the cover design, and to my generous-hearted shipmates in the London Sea Shanty Collective, especially for performing the songs reproduced here. And above all, my deepest gratitude and thanks to my wife, Nony Ardill, and to my children, Anya and Aidan, for their evergreen inspiration, love and support.

Sources

The *Challenger* collection

The photo of sailors on Inaccessible Island is from the *Challenger's* photographic collection at the Royal Maritime Museum, Greenwich. Eileen Brunton's catalogue of *Challenger* photographs is held at the Natural History Museum. The collections amount to a thousand original images of remote seascapes, harbours of tall ships, notables and 'native' populations, and a few of the crew and their brass band.

Crew and scientists' accounts

In parts 1 and 2, I have drawn extensively on Joe's letters and the following accounts of the voyage published by officers and scientists:

At Sea with the Scientifics: The Challenger Letters of Joseph Matkin, ed. Philip F Rehbock (1992)

Log Letters from 'The Challenger', Lord George Granville Campbell (1881)

Notes by a Naturalist Made during the Voyage of HMS 'Challenger', H.N.Moseley (1879)

The Cruise of HMS Challenger: Voyages over many seas, scenes on many lands, W.J.Spry RN(1878)

The Voyage of the Challenger, a personal narrative of the historic circumnavigation of the globe in the years, 1872-1876, Herbert Swire, 1938

Books and web links

The Voyage of the Challenger, Eric Linklater (1972)

The Silent Landscape: The Scientific Voyage of HMS Challenger, James Corfield (2004)

The seabirds cry, Adam Nicholson, (2017)

Before the mast: Naval ratings of the Nineteenth Century, Henry Baynham (1971)

Superior: The return of race science, Angela Saini (2019)

Man Made the City But God Made the Bush: A Detailed History of Early Berowra, Nathan Tilbury, (2016)

Silvertown: The Lost Story of a Strike That Shook London and Helped Launch the Modern Labor Movement, John Tully (2014)

Official reports and sources

The official report of the expedition is referred to in this book as '*Challenger* Report'. The scientific results of the voyage were published in a 50-volume, 29,500-page report taking 23 years to compile. The official title: *Report on the scientific results of the voyage of H.M.S. Challenger during the years 1873-76, under the command of Captain George S. Nares and the late Captain Frank Tourle Thomson.* It was prepared under the superintendence of the late Sir C. Wyville Thomson and then of John Murray.

Available at: www.19thcenturyscience.org/HMSC/HMSC-INDEX/index-linked.htm

Log books and muster books of HMS *Challenger* and HMS *Penelope*: Admiralty records at the National Archives, Kew.

Challenger's Muster book: ADM 117/196. www.discovery. nation- alarchives.gov.uk/details/r/C1745

Charles Collings Certificate of Service: ADM 88/46/64774 and ADM 139/649/24820./

Other sources

Understanding the Oceans, Edited by Margaret Deacon, Tony Rice and Colin Summerhayes, (2001).

Scientists and the Sea (1650-1900), Margaret Deacon (1971).

Oceanographic fame and fortune: The pay of scientists and sailors on the Challenger, Tony Rice (1990), Ocean Challenge, Vol.1 (3), pp. 45-50.

An Anchor in the Unknown: The Exploration and Encounter of HMS Challenger, Erin Yu, www.mdhumanities.org/wp-content/uploads/Yu.HMS*Challenger*-1.pdf

Challenger online collection, www.hmschallenger.net/results

Money, mistakes and the birth of science, www.stem.org.uk/system/files/elibrary-resources/legacy_files_migrated/8428-catalyst_21_2_467.pdf

William Jefford, Boy sailor www.devonheritage.org/Places/Teignmouth/WilliamJefford-thelifeofaVictorianSaliorPage1.htm

Stokers - the lowest of the low? A Social History of Royal Navy Stokers 1850–1950, Dr Tony Chamberlain, www.core.ac.uk/download/pdf/17297620.pdf

The Abolition Project, www.abolition.e2bn.org/slavery_155.html

Emancipation - Black and White, T.H.Huxley (1865) https://mathcs.clarku.edu/huxley/CE3/B&W.html www.mathcs.clarku.edu/huxley/CE3/B&W.html

Submarine cable to Wellington 1876: www.atlantic-cable.com/
Cables/1876Australia-NZ/index.htm

Brighton local history archives are held at The Keep, in
Brighton, including street directories from the 1860s
onwards, local and Sussex county newspaper archives,
coroners' reports and other material.

National census from 1851 onwards.

Songs

A Song for the *Challenger's* Crew

The writer of this song posted to the *Challenger's* crew is anonymous, but the lyrics survive because Joe copied them into his log book. The full nine-verse version is available in *At Sea with the Scientifics*, page 46:

Dedicated to the Best Singer on board
HM Ship *Challenger*

Old David Locker stole our dredge,
To study well its form,
Whilst we were fishing on the Ridge,
Where all his Imps are born.

So never mind your Dredge, my boys,
Which you have lost below;
Our country now your power employs,
That man may wiser grow.

When we have done our work abroad,
And ocean beds and land;
Our Rope, and Dredge, will then afford,
A fact unique and grand.

So never mind your Dredge, my boys,
Which you have lost below;
Our country now your power employs,
That man may wiser grow.

Our mission is to teach the world,
What man ne'er knew before;
All truth by science is unfurl'd
Which nature has in store.

So never mind your Dredge, my boys,
Which you have lost below;
Our country now your power employs,
That man may wiser grow.

'England now expects each man,
His duty to perform;
To carry out our Captain's plan,
The future to adorn.'

So never mind your Dredge, my boys,
Which you have lost below;
Our country now your power employs,
That man may wiser grow

Three cheers my boys, three jolly cheers,
Our captain to inspire;
His glorious staff knows no fears,
Their souls are now on fire.

So never mind your Dredge, my boys,
Which you have lost below;
Our country now your power employs,
That man may wiser grow.

Silvertown

From the 1889 strike at Silver's factories in Silvertown, east London, sprung new unions for working men and women, including the first women's branch of the new National Union of Gasworkers and General Labourers. The London Sea Shanty Collective commemorated the strike with this song, Silvertown, as part of the 2020 Totally Thames Festival. Melody by Ruth Renfrew, lyrics by Philip Pearson.

Back in 1888
First the match girls out the gate.
Then dockers won their tanner,
Now we raise the Silver banner,
Join the union today.

We're marching down to Silver Town,
Early in the morning.
We'll shut old Silver's factory down,
A new day is dawning.

Plantation rubber rolls up river,
Up the Thames to Mr Silver.
Now we slave on the factory floor,
70 hours a week – No more!
Join the union today.

We're marching down to Silver Town,
Early in the morning.
We'll shut old Silver's factory down,
A new day is dawning.

Farthings more is all we ask
For the rubber melt and furnace blast.
Women getting equal pay,
Send the blacklegs on their way,
Join the union today.

We're marching down to Silver Town,
Early in the morning.
We'll shut old Silver's factory down,
A new day is dawning.

Sugar and spice and all things nice
They come rolling up the river.
And rubber and tar they ain't so nice,
Send old Silver down the river.
Join the union today.

We're marching down to Silver Town,
Early in the morning.
We'll shut old Silver's factory down,
A new day is dawning.

Ten thousand march to Vicky Park
We go marching in the morning,
With a fife and drum and Eleanor Marx,
We see a new day dawning,
Join the union today.

Silvertown

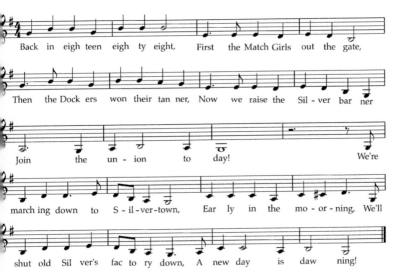

Back in eigh teen eigh ty eight, First the Match Girls out the gate,

Then the Dock ers won their tan ner, Now we raise the Sil - ver bar ner

Join the un - ion to day! We're

march ing down to S - il - ver-town, Ear ly in the mo - or - ning, We'll

shut old Sil ver's fac to ry down, A new day is daw ning!

Valparaiso

Honolulu, July 28 1875. After three long years at sea, Joe Matkin wrote in a letter home: *'The mail is in, and there is not a single letter or newspaper for me from anyone; now I shall have to wait until we reach Valparaiso in November...it is nearly a twelve-month since I heard from you or the boys. If you have any bad news to tell, it is better to tell it at once, than leave people to "think and fear". I suppose I shall get a heavy mail in Valparaiso, but we shan't be there for three months yet.'*

Listening to me trying out this song as we were returning home from the park one day, Nony said it needed a chorus, like all shanties do. So, as we walked, Nony gifted the song a chorus and its melody.

Lyrics and melody: Philip Pearson and Nony Ardill.
Arrangement: Maggie Boyd and Benni Lees-MacPherson.

Valparaiso

Pacific Ocean, vast and wide,
Vast and wide
No sail in sight, sail in sight,
Nor bird's eye, No word from home until they dock,
No word from home until they dock, No word from
home until they dock at Valparaiso.

It's been three long years as sea.
Will you remember me,
Like I remember you?
Will you remember me?

VERSE TWO
And the men stand restless on the deck,
Restless on deck,
As the purser cuts into the letter sack,
Letter sack
Names a man for whom the waiting
Names a man for whom the waiting,
Names a man for whom the waiting now is ending.

Been three long years as sea.
Will you remember me,
Like I remember you?
Will you remember me?

So that brave and fearless man,
Fearless man
No seaman's task beyond his hand,
Beyond his hand,
Now grips upon on his prize
Now grips upon on his prize,
Now grips upon on his prize to hide the trembling.

Been three long years as sea.
Will you remember me,
Like I remember you?
Will you remember me?

With his longed for letter home,
Letter home,
He hurries off, must be alone,
Must be alone,
Alone with words to carry him home,
Alone with words to carry him home,
Alone with words to see him home or ease a longing,
Ease his longing.

Been three long years as sea.
Will you remember me,
Like I remember you?
Will you remember me?

Turkey Bones

Philip Pearson

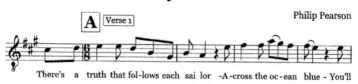

There's a truth that fol-lows each sai lor -A-cross the oc-ean blue - You'll

ne -ver get fat on a sai -lor's tuck less you nicks a bit more forthe crew

We was five days out from Pom pey And al-read-y get -ting thin-ner When

some-bo-dy ni-cked the tur-key all dressed for the off -i -cers' Christ-mas day

din-ner. There was a hell of a hal-la-ba - loo, cap-tain roar-ing like a

ga - le They found tur - key bones and a

nice pinch of salt tucked a - way in the top gal-lant sa - il.

Turkey Bones

This song is inspired by a hungry sailor. In one of Joe's first letters home after leaving Portsmouth (or 'Pompey', as sailors called it), he writes that a roast turkey had gone missing from the officer's table. 'I'd have liked to pick a bit off that turkey myself. I have never been so hungry as the last few days. It's a regular man-o'-war diet now we're on. And us only sporting a pair of cannon.' The song was 'premiered' by the London Sea Shanty Collective on Greenland Dock during the 2019 Totally Thames Festival accompanied by gobbles, hinks and quacks.

Lyrics: Philip Pearson.
Arrangement: Maggie Boyd and Jane Perrot.

Turkey Bones

There's a truth that follows each sailor,
Across the ocean blue
You'll never get fat on a sailor's tuck,
'Less we nicks a bit more for the crew.

We was five days out from Pompey
And already getting thinner,
When somebody nicked the Turkey all dressed
For the officers' Christmas Day dinner.

There was a hell of a hallaballoo
Captain roaring like a gale,
They found Turkey bones and a nice pinch of salt
Tucked away in the topgallant sail.

We was six days out from Pompey
And still we're getting thinner,
When somebody nicked the Goose all dressed,
For the officers' Boxing Day dinner.

There was a hell of a hallaballoo
Captain roaring for his supper,
They found Goos-e's bones and a nice pinch of salt
Tucked away in the old packet's scuppers.

Well, we was nine days out from Pompey
And getting thinner & thinner,
When somebody nicked the Ducks all dressed,
For the officers' New Year's Day dinner.

There was a hell of a hallaballoo
Captain singing the same old carol,
They found the Duck's bones and a nice pinch of salt
Tucked away in the ten-pounder's barrel.

So here's to that poor hungry sailor,
Just one of Challenger crew,
He never got fat in his purse or his paunch,
And bejazuss neither would you.

Author's Biography

Philip Pearson grew up in Brighton, within sight of the sea. He studied geography at college and developed a lifelong interest in environmental issues. This drew him to the fascinating story of the voyage of the *Challenger* and its astonishing achievements.

Philip Pearson.

He worked in the trade union movement for much of his life. He has published two books reflecting much of this work: *Twilight robber: trade unions and low paid workers* (1986) and *Keeping Well at Work* (2004).

The idea for a narrative of the life of his great grandfather, Charlie Collins, one of the *Challenger's* crew, was inspired by the creative writing classes at the Mary Ward Centre, London.

He sings with the London Sea Shanty Collective choir, and the narrative is doubtless influenced by the stories and rhythms of these working songs of the sea. Philip and his wife Nony, who passed away in 2021, have two children, Anya and Aidan.